First published in 2023 by Hungry Tomato Ltd.
F15, Old Bakery Studios, Blewetts Wharf,
Malpas Road, Truro, Cornwall, TR1 1QH, UK.

Thanks to our creative team:
Senior Editor: Anna Hussey
Graphic Designer: Amy Harvey

A CIP catalog record for this book is available from the British Library.

ISBN: 978-1-915461-14-8

Printed and bound in China

Discover more at
www.hungrytomato.com
www.mybeetlebooks.com

# D🐾GS

## An illustrated guide to 100 brilliant breeds!

By Annabel Griffin

Illustrated by Marina Halak

# CONTENTS

## Wonderful Working Dogs

## Super-skilled Dogs

## Cuddly Companions

## Pawsome Pup Awards

Words in **bold** can be found in the glossary.

# THE WORLD OF DOGS

Get ready to explore the wonderful world of dogs! From the tiny chihuahua to the giant Irish wolfhound, there are so many different types of lovable dogs to discover.

Big or small, they've got it all!

wolf or dog? who knows.

## WHERE DO DOGS COME FROM?

Believe it or not, all dogs are **descendants** of ancient wolves. The details of how and when wolves became dogs are still quite foggy, but it likely started when humans began to **domesticate** and train wolves, at least 14,000 years ago. Today, dogs can be found all over the world.

# WHAT IS A BREED?

A breed is a particular group of dogs that all share the same (or very similar) appearance and characteristics, making them easy to identify. There are hundreds of different breeds, and they can vary wildly in size, shape, hairiness and personality.

Not all dogs belong to a specific breed. Some dogs, known as mutts or mongrels, are a mixture of lots of different breeds. They can make fantastic and unique pets, and can often be found looking for a loving home at rescue or **rehoming shelters.**

They're all so cute, though.

# GETTING A DOG?

Maybe you already have a dog in your family, or maybe you'd like to in the future. Owning a dog can be fun and rewarding, but it's also a big responsibility. Some dogs need a lot of space, time and attention. Before buying or adopting a dog, you should always carefully research their breed and think about whether you are able to give them everything they need to be happy.

Not all dogs are as chilled out as this one!

# BREED GROUPS

Dog breeds are often arranged into seven different groups that are loosely based on the jobs that they were originally bred to do.

## SPORTING GROUP

Also known as gundogs, they were originally bred to help hunters retrieve birds.

## NON-SPORTING GROUP

This is the group for dogs that don't fit into any of the other groups, so they are quite a mixed bunch!

## TERRIER GROUP

This group were originally bred to hunt burrowing animals, such as rats, rabbits, foxes, and badgers. Most of them have "terrier" as part of their name.

## WORKING GROUP

Dogs in this group were originally bred to perform practical tasks, such as pulling sleds and carts. They were also often used as watchdogs. They are usually large dogs.

**SIGHTHOUNDS**
These dogs are usually
long, lean and very fast.

**SCENT HOUNDS**
These dogs have droopy
ears and powerful noses.

# HOUND GROUP

Hounds were bred for their sense of smell or sight, and were usually used for hunting. They can be split into two sub-groups: sighthounds and scent hounds.

# HERDING GROUP

This group includes dogs that were bred to work on farms, herding and guarding livestock, such as sheep and cows.

# TOY GROUP

Tiny breeds that are small enough to sit in your lap fall into this group. They are bred mostly as pets and companions.

# WONDERFUL WORKING DOGS

Dogs and humans have been working side by side for thousands of years. Many breeds of dog have been designed to be good at specific jobs, such as herding, hunting and guarding.

Most working dog breeds have a high level of intelligence, energy, and trainability. They can be loyal and loving companions but often require more time and attention than dogs bred purely for companionship.

# Border Collie

Bursting with energy and intelligence, border collies are famous for being excellent sheepdogs. They are very loyal and easy to train, but can become bored easily and need a lot of daily exercise.

Playful people-pleaser

Athletic body

Hard-working

Thick coat

**ORIGIN:** United Kingdom

**COAT:** Medium-length, smooth

**PERSONALITY:** Smart and hard-working

**MEDIUM**

INTELLIGENCE

ENERGY LEVEL

TRAINABILITY

# Old English Sheepdog

These giant balls of fluff make great sheepdogs and have even been known to try and herd children! They are friendly, love to explore, and make great walking companions. Their thick coats need a lot of grooming. Some owners actually shave their dog's fur and spin it into yarn!

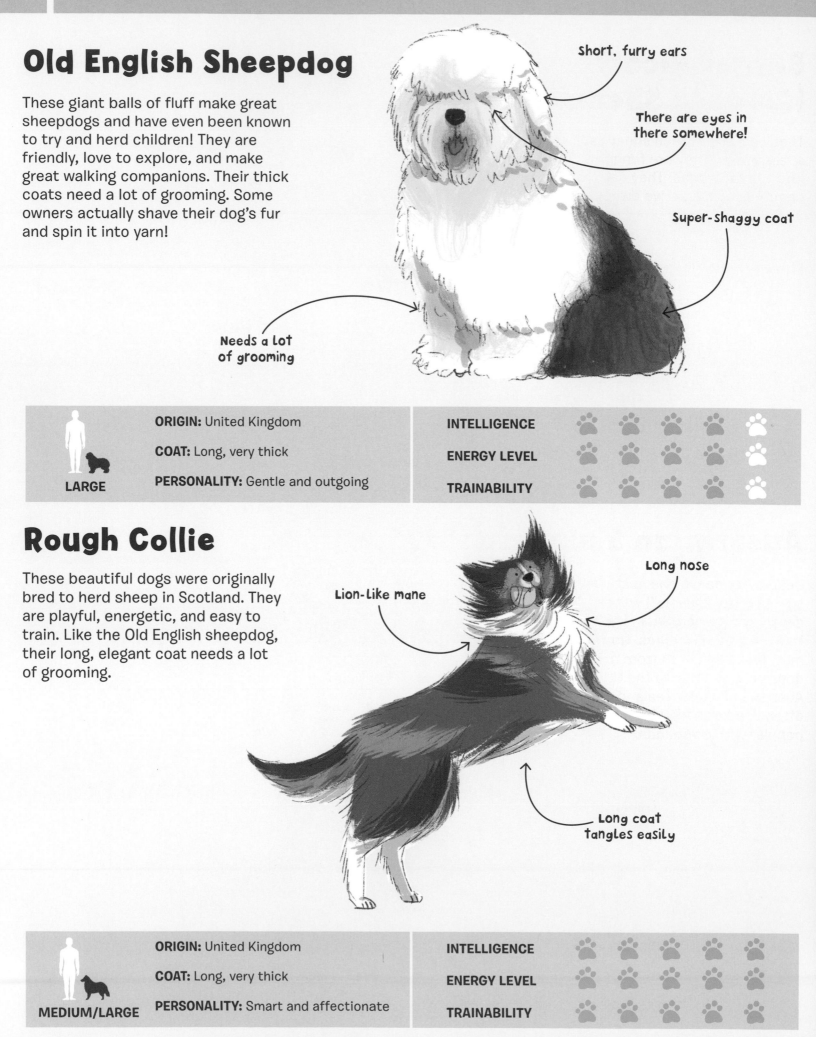

Short, furry ears

There are eyes in there somewhere!

Super-shaggy coat

Needs a lot of grooming

| | | |
|---|---|---|
| **LARGE** | **ORIGIN:** United Kingdom | |
| | **COAT:** Long, very thick | |
| | **PERSONALITY:** Gentle and outgoing | |

INTELLIGENCE 🐾🐾🐾🐾🐾

ENERGY LEVEL 🐾🐾🐾🐾🐾

TRAINABILITY 🐾🐾🐾🐾🐾

# Rough Collie

These beautiful dogs were originally bred to herd sheep in Scotland. They are playful, energetic, and easy to train. Like the Old English sheepdog, their long, elegant coat needs a lot of grooming.

Lion-like mane

Long nose

Long coat tangles easily

| | | |
|---|---|---|
| **MEDIUM/LARGE** | **ORIGIN:** United Kingdom | |
| | **COAT:** Long, very thick | |
| | **PERSONALITY:** Smart and affectionate | |

INTELLIGENCE 🐾🐾🐾🐾🐾

ENERGY LEVEL 🐾🐾🐾🐾🐾

TRAINABILITY 🐾🐾🐾🐾🐾

# Berger Picard (Picardy Sheepdog)

These scruffy French sheepdogs are now a rare breed. They are funny and loyal, and love to play games. They can make excellent companions for active owners.

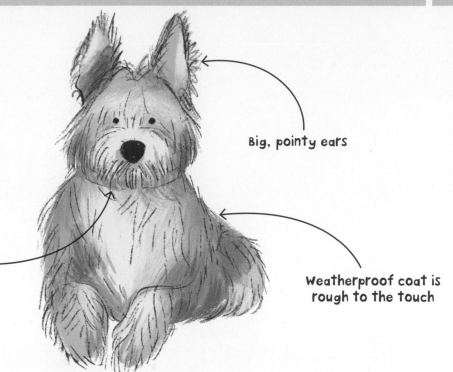

Big, pointy ears

Scruffy beard and eyebrows

Weatherproof coat is rough to the touch

**MEDIUM**

**ORIGIN:** France

**COAT:** Medium-length, **wiry**

**PERSONALITY:** Playful but sensitive

INTELLIGENCE

ENERGY LEVEL

TRAINABILITY

# Australian Shepherd

Despite its name, the Australian shepherd (or "Aussie") was actually developed in the USA, in the 1800s, to work on the **ranches**. However, it may have been bred from herding dogs brought over to the USA from Australia and New Zealand. It is still often used as a working dog and is popular with cowhands.

Eyes can be brown, blue, amber, or a combination of shades.

Bushy tail

Smiley face

**MEDIUM**

**ORIGIN:** USA

**COAT:** Medium-length, thick

**PERSONALITY:** Active and protective

INTELLIGENCE

ENERGY LEVEL

TRAINABILITY

# Standard Schnauzer

Schnauzers were originally bred as multipurpose farm dogs, with good skills in guarding livestock and rat-catching. They are very intelligent, alert and protective, making them good watchdogs.

straight back

Bushy eyebrows

Bearded snout

**MEDIUM**

**ORIGIN:** Germany

**COAT:** Medium-length, wiry

**PERSONALITY:** Lively and alert

| INTELLIGENCE | 🐾 🐾 🐾 🐾 🐾 |
| --- | --- |
| ENERGY LEVEL | 🐾 🐾 🐾 🐾 🐾 |
| TRAINABILITY | 🐾 🐾 🐾 🐾 🐾 |

# Puli

Is it a dog or is it a mop? This unusual-looking breed was originally used as a herding dog by the **nomadic** Magyar tribes, who settled in what is now Hungary in the 9th century CE. They make great family pets, but their amazing long coats need a lot of looking after.

Shiny, black nose

Speedy and acrobatic

Long, corded coat

**MEDIUM**

**ORIGIN:** Hungary

**COAT:** Long, **corded**

**PERSONALITY:** Fun-loving and friendly

| INTELLIGENCE | 🐾 🐾 🐾 🐾 🐾 |
| --- | --- |
| ENERGY LEVEL | 🐾 🐾 🐾 🐾 🐾 |
| TRAINABILITY | 🐾 🐾 🐾 🐾 🐾 |

# Pembrokeshire Welsh Corgi

These dogs are famous for being the beloved pets of Queen Elizabeth II of the United Kingdom, but they were originally bred as cattle-herders and guard dogs in Wales. Despite their short legs, they are surprisingly speedy and athletic.

Fox-like face

Big, pointy ears

Long body

Short but powerful legs

**SMALL/MEDIUM**

**ORIGIN:** United Kingdom

**COAT:** Medium-length, thick

**PERSONALITY:** Loving but independent

INTELLIGENCE

ENERGY LEVEL

TRAINABILITY

# Belgian Shepherd

This hard-working breed are more than just great herding dogs. Belgian shepherds are used for a variety of other jobs, including as **service dogs**, guard dogs and police and military dogs.

Bright eyes

Bushy tail

Shiny coat

**LARGE**

**ORIGIN:** Belgium

**COAT:** Long, thick

**PERSONALITY:** Brave and loyal

INTELLIGENCE

ENERGY LEVEL

TRAINABILITY

# German Shepherd

One of the most popular working breeds, the German shepherd is a brilliant all-rounder. As the name suggests, they were originally German herding dogs, but can tackle just about any job a dog can do. They are often used for police work, search-and-rescue, and are even taken into war zones by the military. They also make good companion and service dogs, and are popular pets.

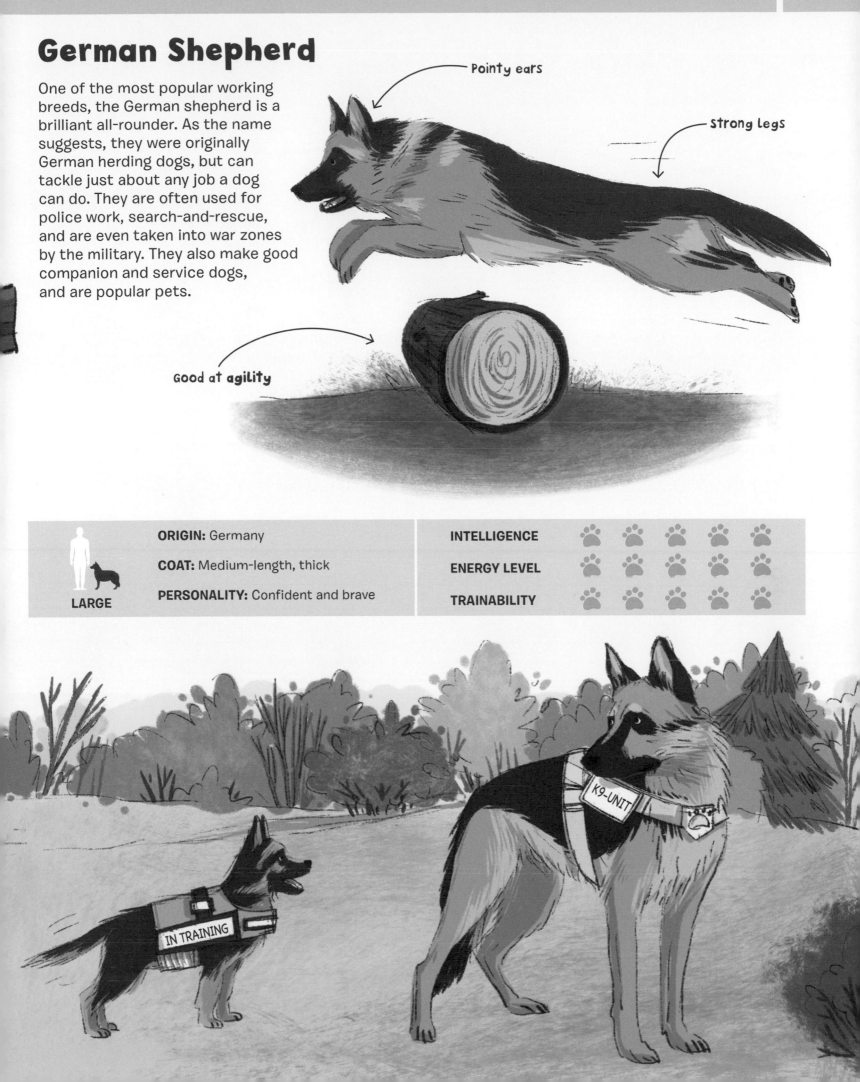

Pointy ears

Strong legs

Good at agility

| | | |
|---|---|---|
| **LARGE** | **ORIGIN:** Germany | |
| | **COAT:** Medium-length, thick | |
| | **PERSONALITY:** Confident and brave | |

| | | | | | |
|---|---|---|---|---|---|
| **INTELLIGENCE** | 🐾 | 🐾 | 🐾 | 🐾 | 🐾 |
| **ENERGY LEVEL** | 🐾 | 🐾 | 🐾 | 🐾 | 🐾 |
| **TRAINABILITY** | 🐾 | 🐾 | 🐾 | 🐾 | 🐾 |

IN TRAINING

K9-UNIT

# Siberian Husky

This well-known dog was first bred by the Chukchi people of Siberia to pull sleds and for companionship. They are strong dogs, with incredible **endurance** for running long distances in difficult conditions. They are popular pets, but their high-energy, mischievous nature can make them quite a handful!

Loud howler

often have piercing blue eyes

Thick coat to keep warm in freezing conditions

Wolf-like appearance

| | | |
|---|---|---|
| **MEDIUM/LARGE** | **ORIGIN:** Siberia | |
| | **COAT:** Medium-length, very thick | |
| | **PERSONALITY:** Friendly and mischievous | |

| | |
|---|---|
| INTELLIGENCE | 🐾🐾🐾🐾🐾 |
| ENERGY LEVEL | 🐾🐾🐾🐾🐾 |
| TRAINABILITY | 🐾🐾🐾🐾🐾 |

Sled dogs have been used for transport in the Arctic for thousands of years, but these days they are mostly used for leisure and racing events.

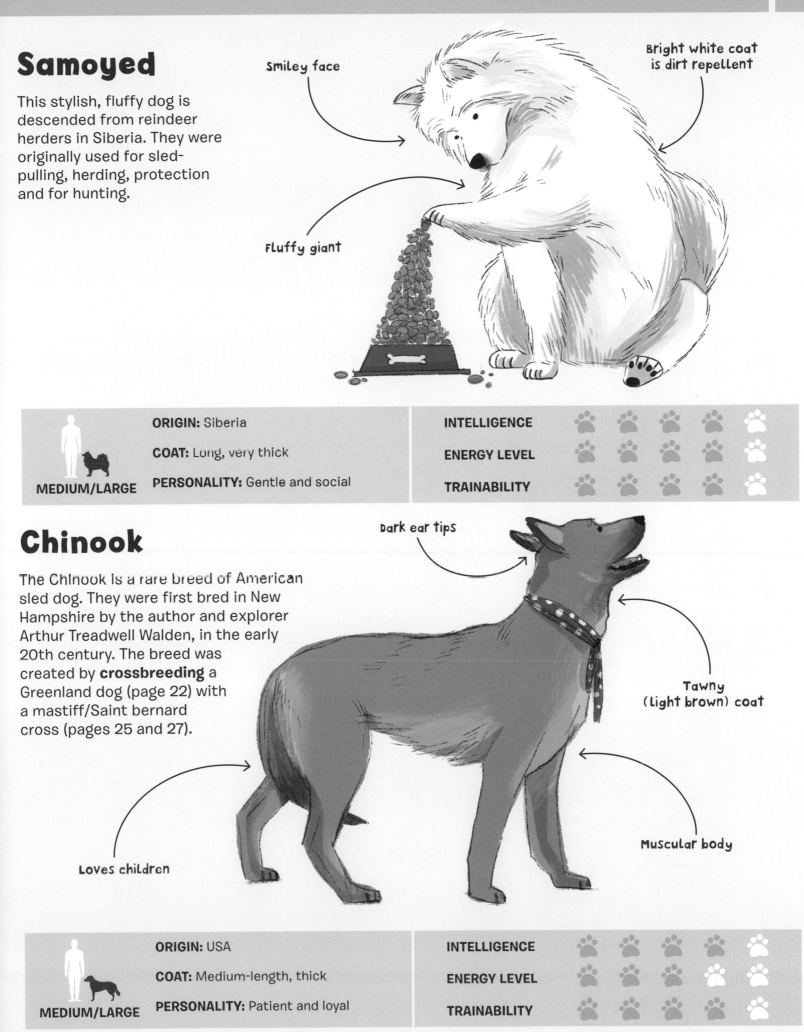

# Samoyed

This stylish, fluffy dog is descended from reindeer herders in Siberia. They were originally used for sled-pulling, herding, protection and for hunting.

Smiley face

Bright white coat is dirt repellent

Fluffy giant

**ORIGIN:** Siberia

**COAT:** Long, very thick

**PERSONALITY:** Gentle and social

MEDIUM/LARGE

INTELLIGENCE

ENERGY LEVEL

TRAINABILITY

# Chinook

The Chinook is a rare breed of American sled dog. They were first bred in New Hampshire by the author and explorer Arthur Treadwell Walden, in the early 20th century. The breed was created by **crossbreeding** a Greenland dog (page 22) with a mastiff/Saint bernard cross (pages 25 and 27).

Dark ear tips

Tawny (light brown) coat

Muscular body

Loves children

**ORIGIN:** USA

**COAT:** Medium-length, thick

**PERSONALITY:** Patient and loyal

MEDIUM/LARGE

INTELLIGENCE

ENERGY LEVEL

TRAINABILITY

# Alaskan Malamute

Although they bear many similarities, the Alaskan malamute is bigger, stronger and fluffier than its close relative, the Siberian husky (page 20). Malamutes are also slower, however. They were bred to carry heavy loads over long distances.

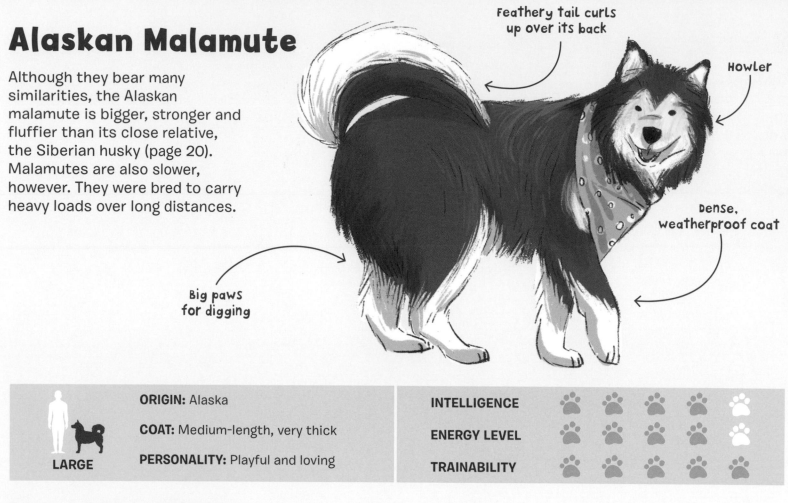

Feathery tail curls up over its back

Howler

Dense, weatherproof coat

Big paws for digging

| | ORIGIN: Alaska | | INTELLIGENCE | 🐾 🐾 🐾 🐾 🐾 |
|---|---|---|---|---|
| LARGE | COAT: Medium-length, very thick | | ENERGY LEVEL | 🐾 🐾 🐾 🐾 🐾 |
| | PERSONALITY: Playful and loving | | TRAINABILITY | 🐾 🐾 🐾 🐾 🐾 🐾 |

# Greenland Dog

The Greenland dog is an ancient sled dog breed, which is thought to have changed very little since it was brought to Greenland from Siberia by the Thule people 1,000 years ago. **Genetically,** it is now considered the same breed as the Canadian Eskimo dog.

Wide head

A rare breed

Tail is usually rolled along/across its back

| | ORIGIN: Greenland | | INTELLIGENCE | 🐾 🐾 🐾 🐾 🐾 |
|---|---|---|---|---|
| LARGE | COAT: Medium-length, very thick | | ENERGY LEVEL | 🐾 🐾 🐾 🐾 🐾 |
| | PERSONALITY: Loyal and good-natured | | TRAINABILITY | 🐾 🐾 🐾 🐾 🐾 |

# Bernese Mountain Dog

These dogs were bred to pull carts in the Swiss Alps. They were also used as farm dogs. They are gentle giants who love being outdoors.

Big, powerful body

Black and tan markings

White chest

**ORIGIN:** Switzerland

**COAT:** Long, thick

**PERSONALITY:** Calm and strong

LARGE/EXTRA LARGE

INTELLIGENCE

ENERGY LEVEL

TRAINABILITY

# Bouvier des Flandres

This big, shaggy dog started out as a farm dog in Flanders, Belgium. It was used for herding and pulling carts. They also make excellent guard and watchdogs.

could use a haircut!

Big beard

Thick, weatherproof coat

Needs a lot of grooming

**ORIGIN:** Belgium

**COAT:** Medium-length, thick, wavy

**PERSONALITY:** Fearless and independent

LARGE/EXTRA LARGE

INTELLIGENCE

ENERGY LEVEL

TRAINABILITY

# Rottweiler

The size, obedience and fearlessness of Rottweiler's, makes them excellent guard and security dogs. They may look intimidating, but they can be gentle and loving family pets. They can also have a very playful, silly side.

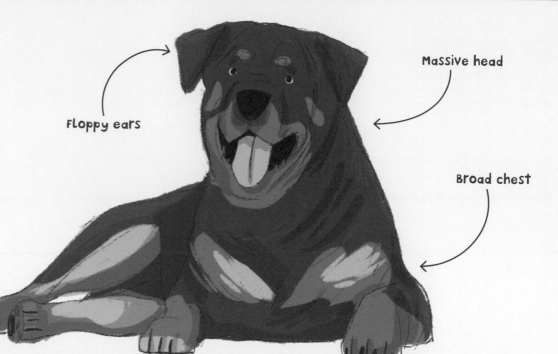

Floppy ears

Massive head

Broad chest

**LARGE/EXTRA LARGE**

**ORIGIN:** Germany

**COAT:** Short, smooth

**PERSONALITY:** Gentle and obedient

| INTELLIGENCE | 🐾 🐾 🐾 🐾 🐾 |
| ENERGY LEVEL | 🐾 🐾 🐾 🐾 🐾 |
| TRAINABILITY | 🐾 🐾 🐾 🐾 🐾 |

# Boxer

Boxers were originally bred as hunting dogs in the 19th century. They are strong, alert, and suspicious of strangers, making them great guard dogs. They are very affectionate with their owners.

Wrinkled forehead

Sad-looking eyes

Lower jaw sticks out further than upper jaw (underbite)

White socks

**MEDIUM/LARGE**

**ORIGIN:** Germany

**COAT:** Short, smooth

**PERSONALITY:** Fun-loving and alert

| INTELLIGENCE | 🐾 🐾 🐾 🐾 🐾 |
| ENERGY LEVEL | 🐾 🐾 🐾 🐾 🐾 |
| TRAINABILITY | 🐾 🐾 🐾 🐾 🐾 |

# Great Dane

Great Danes are one of the largest breeds of dog and can measure up to 35 inches (90 cm) in height. It's no wonder they make good guard dogs, since their size could scare off any intruder! Don't be fooled, though; they're really gentle giants.

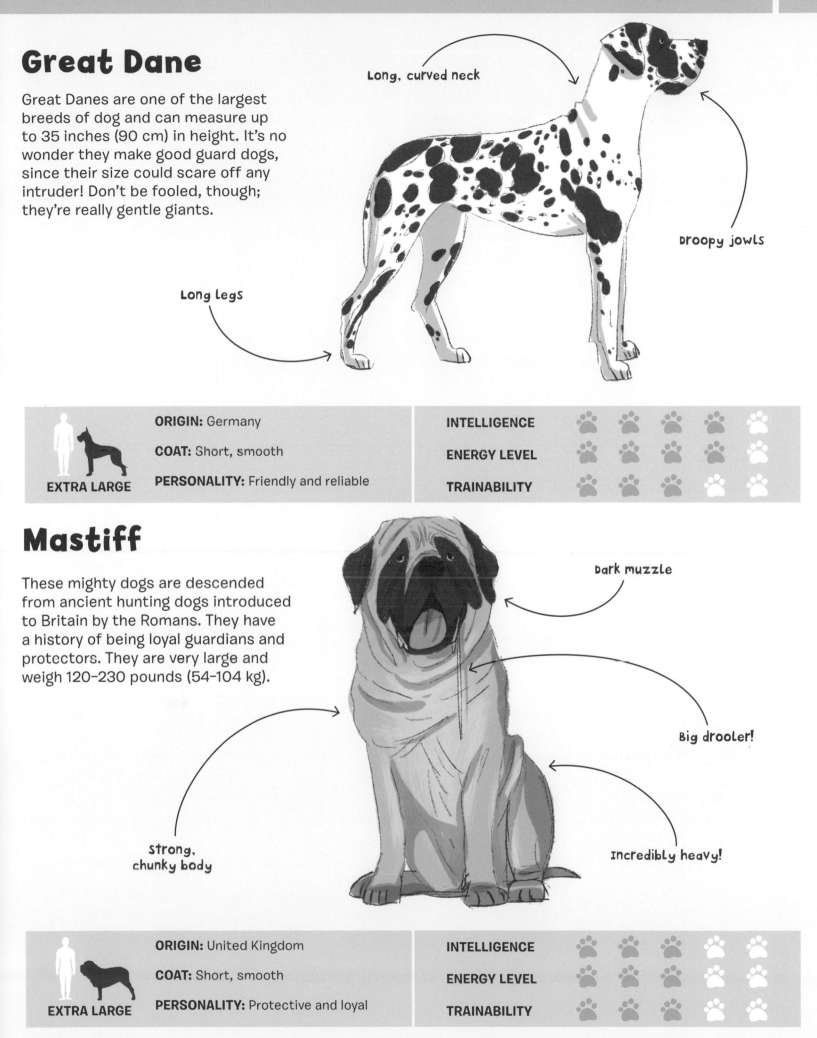

Long, curved neck

Droopy jowls

Long legs

**EXTRA LARGE**

**ORIGIN:** Germany

**COAT:** Short, smooth

**PERSONALITY:** Friendly and reliable

INTELLIGENCE

ENERGY LEVEL

TRAINABILITY

# Mastiff

These mighty dogs are descended from ancient hunting dogs introduced to Britain by the Romans. They have a history of being loyal guardians and protectors. They are very large and weigh 120–230 pounds (54–104 kg).

Dark muzzle

Big drooler!

Incredibly heavy!

Strong, chunky body

**EXTRA LARGE**

**ORIGIN:** United Kingdom

**COAT:** Short, smooth

**PERSONALITY:** Protective and loyal

INTELLIGENCE

ENERGY LEVEL

TRAINABILITY

# Dobermann (Doberman Pinscher)

This breed have brilliant guarding and tracking skills. They are also speedy and very intelligent. It's no wonder they make good police dogs! They love being part of an active family.

Pointy snout

Sleek and elegant

Shiny, black and tan coat

**LARGE**

**ORIGIN:** Germany

**COAT:** Short, smooth

**PERSONALITY:** Alert and fearless

| INTELLIGENCE | 🐾 🐾 🐾 🐾 🐾 |
| ENERGY LEVEL | 🐾 🐾 🐾 🐾 🐾 |
| TRAINABILITY | 🐾 🐾 🐾 🐾 🐾 |

# Airedale Terrier

Sometimes called 'The King of the Terriers', Airedales are the largest of the terrier breeds (see page 10). They were originally bred for hunting, but have a strong history as police and military dogs. In World War I, they were used to carry messages to soldiers behind enemy lines.

Long, flat head

Bearded muzzle

Black saddle markings

**MEDIUM/LARGE**

**ORIGIN:** United Kingdom

**COAT:** Short/medium-length, wiry

**PERSONALITY:** Sporty and determined

| INTELLIGENCE | 🐾 🐾 🐾 🐾 🐾 |
| ENERGY LEVEL | 🐾 🐾 🐾 🐾 🐾 |
| TRAINABILITY | 🐾 🐾 🐾 🐾 🐾 |

# Saint Bernard

This massive breed was originally bred by the monks of the Great Saint Bernard Hospice in the Swiss Alps as guard dogs, but were later used for mountain rescue. They can often face difficult and dangerous conditions to rescue people lost in the mountains.

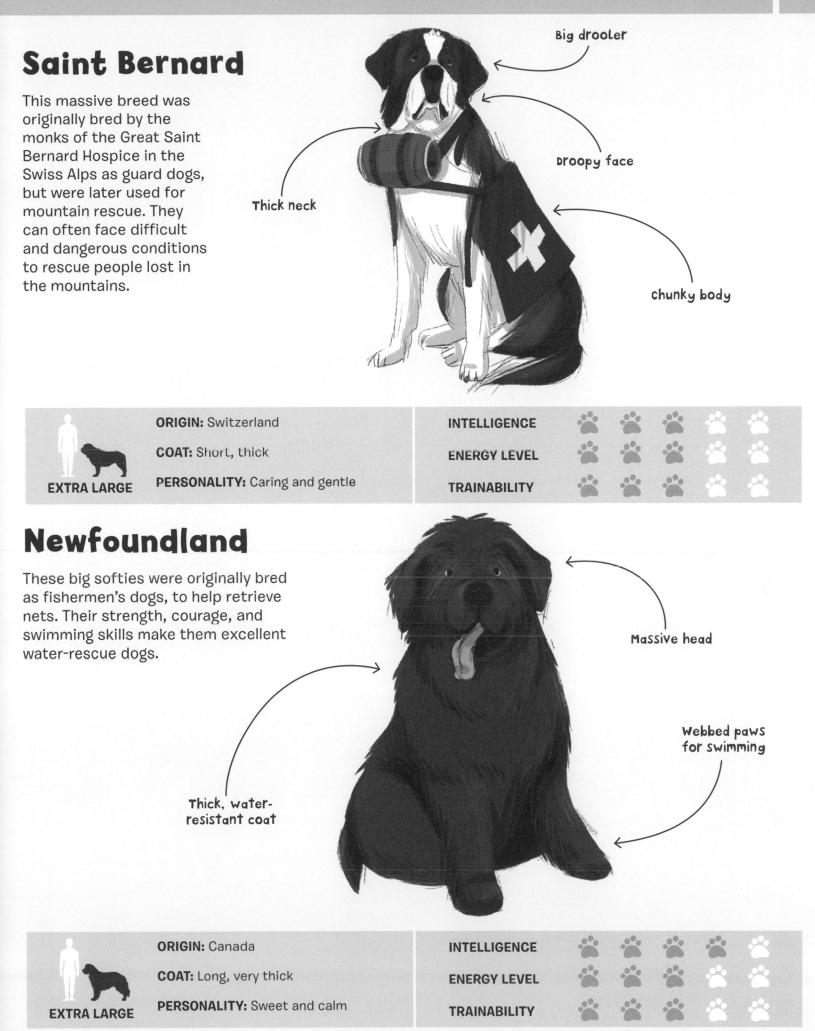

Big drooler

Droopy face

Thick neck

chunky body

**ORIGIN:** Switzerland

**COAT:** Short, thick

**PERSONALITY:** Caring and gentle

EXTRA LARGE

| INTELLIGENCE | | | | | |
| --- | --- | --- | --- | --- | --- |
| ENERGY LEVEL | | | | | |
| TRAINABILITY | | | | | |

# Newfoundland

These big softies were originally bred as fishermen's dogs, to help retrieve nets. Their strength, courage, and swimming skills make them excellent water-rescue dogs.

Massive head

Webbed paws for swimming

Thick, water-resistant coat

**ORIGIN:** Canada

**COAT:** Long, very thick

**PERSONALITY:** Sweet and calm

EXTRA LARGE

| INTELLIGENCE | | | | | |
| --- | --- | --- | --- | --- | --- |
| ENERGY LEVEL | | | | | |
| TRAINABILITY | | | | | |

# SUPER-SKILLED DOGS

There are some really talented dogs out there! While all dogs are amazing, some breeds are particularly skilled at certain things. Some have incredible noses, capable of sniffing out scents from miles away. Others are incredibly speedy, great at fetch, or clever climbers. Many of these skills are useful for performing particular jobs or tasks, but they can also be a lot of fun!

# Bloodhound

The bloodhound has the strongest sense of smell of any dog breed. With their super noses and excellent tracking skills, they are often used by police detectives to help solve crimes and find missing people.

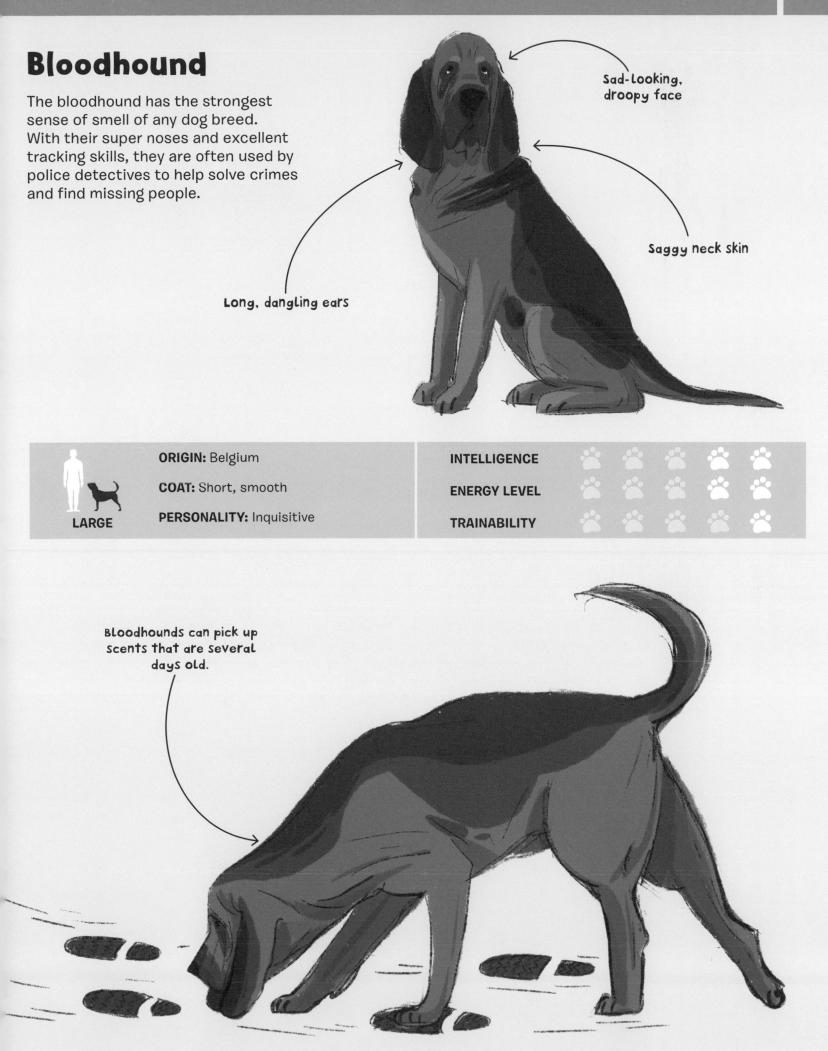

Sad-looking, droopy face

Saggy neck skin

Long, dangling ears

| | ORIGIN: Belgium | INTELLIGENCE | 🐾 🐾 🐾 🐾 🐾 |
|---|---|---|---|
| | COAT: Short, smooth | ENERGY LEVEL | 🐾 🐾 🐾 🐾 🐾 |
| LARGE | PERSONALITY: Inquisitive | TRAINABILITY | 🐾 🐾 🐾 🐾 🐾 |

Bloodhounds can pick up scents that are several days old.

# Basset Hound

The basset hound's sense of smell is second only to the bloodhound. Its long, floppy ears help to trap smells and waft them towards its nose.

Surprisingly heavy

Resting sad face

Droopy ears

Stubby legs

| | | INTELLIGENCE | |
|---|---|---|---|
|  **MEDIUM** | **ORIGIN:** United Kingdom<br>**COAT:** Short, smooth<br>**PERSONALITY:** Friendly and easy-going | **INTELLIGENCE**<br>**ENERGY LEVEL**<br>**TRAINABILITY** | 🐾🐾🐾🐾🐾<br>🐾🐾🐾🐾🐾<br>🐾🐾🐾🐾🐾 |

# American Foxhound

These dogs were one of the first breeds to be developed in the United States, and were even bred by President George Washington. However, they are now one of the rarest breeds in the country.

Large brown/ hazel eyes

Long nose

Strong legs

| | | | |
|---|---|---|---|
| **MEDIUM** | **ORIGIN:** USA<br>**COAT:** Short, smooth<br>**PERSONALITY:** Kind and gentle | **INTELLIGENCE**<br>**ENERGY LEVEL**<br>**TRAINABILITY** | 🐾🐾🐾🐾🐾<br>🐾🐾🐾🐾🐾<br>🐾🐾🐾🐾🐾 |

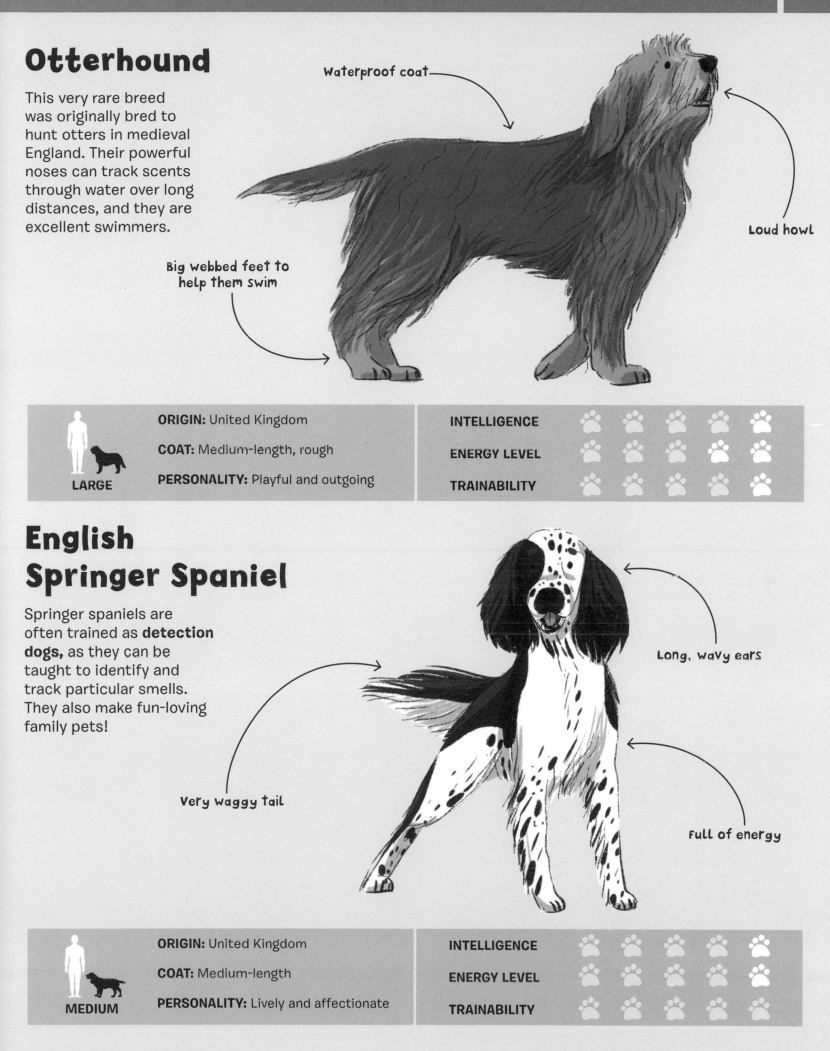

# Otterhound

This very rare breed was originally bred to hunt otters in medieval England. Their powerful noses can track scents through water over long distances, and they are excellent swimmers.

Waterproof coat

Loud howl

Big webbed feet to help them swim

| | | |
|---|---|---|
| **LARGE** | **ORIGIN:** United Kingdom | |
| | **COAT:** Medium-length, rough | |
| | **PERSONALITY:** Playful and outgoing | |

| INTELLIGENCE | 🐾 🐾 🐾 🐾 🐾 |
|---|---|
| ENERGY LEVEL | 🐾 🐾 🐾 🐾 🐾 |
| TRAINABILITY | 🐾 🐾 🐾 🐾 🐾 |

# English Springer Spaniel

Springer spaniels are often trained as **detection dogs,** as they can be taught to identify and track particular smells. They also make fun-loving family pets!

Long, wavy ears

Very waggy tail

Full of energy

| | | |
|---|---|---|
| **MEDIUM** | **ORIGIN:** United Kingdom | |
| | **COAT:** Medium-length | |
| | **PERSONALITY:** Lively and affectionate | |

| INTELLIGENCE | 🐾 🐾 🐾 🐾 🐾 |
|---|---|
| ENERGY LEVEL | 🐾 🐾 🐾 🐾 🐾 |
| TRAINABILITY | 🐾 🐾 🐾 🐾 🐾 |

# Beagle

These small hounds were first bred for hunting, but have also become popular pets. They are sometimes used as detection dogs, trained to sniff out drugs, explosives and other illegal items.

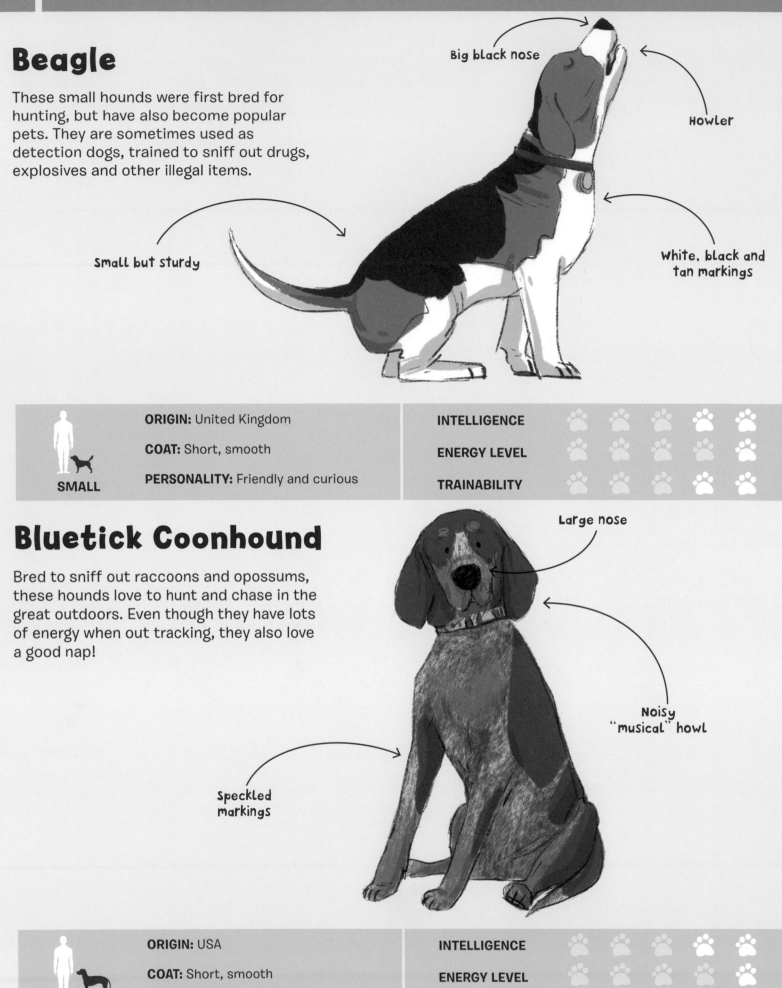

Big black nose

Howler

Small but sturdy

white, black and tan markings

| | | | |
|---|---|---|---|
| **SMALL** | **ORIGIN:** United Kingdom | **INTELLIGENCE** | 🐾🐾🐾🐾🐾 |
| | **COAT:** Short, smooth | **ENERGY LEVEL** | 🐾🐾🐾🐾🐾 |
| | **PERSONALITY:** Friendly and curious | **TRAINABILITY** | 🐾🐾🐾🐾🐾 |

# Bluetick Coonhound

Bred to sniff out raccoons and opossums, these hounds love to hunt and chase in the great outdoors. Even though they have lots of energy when out tracking, they also love a good nap!

Large nose

Noisy "musical" howl

Speckled markings

| | | | |
|---|---|---|---|
| **LARGE** | **ORIGIN:** USA | **INTELLIGENCE** | 🐾🐾🐾🐾🐾 |
| | **COAT:** Short, smooth | **ENERGY LEVEL** | 🐾🐾🐾🐾🐾 |
| | **PERSONALITY:** Friendly and curious | **TRAINABILITY** | 🐾🐾🐾🐾🐾 |

# Lagotto Romagnolo

These adorable curly-coated pups are known for making great **truffle** hounds in Italy. Their strong sense of smell helps them to sniff out rare, valuable truffles buried in the ground.

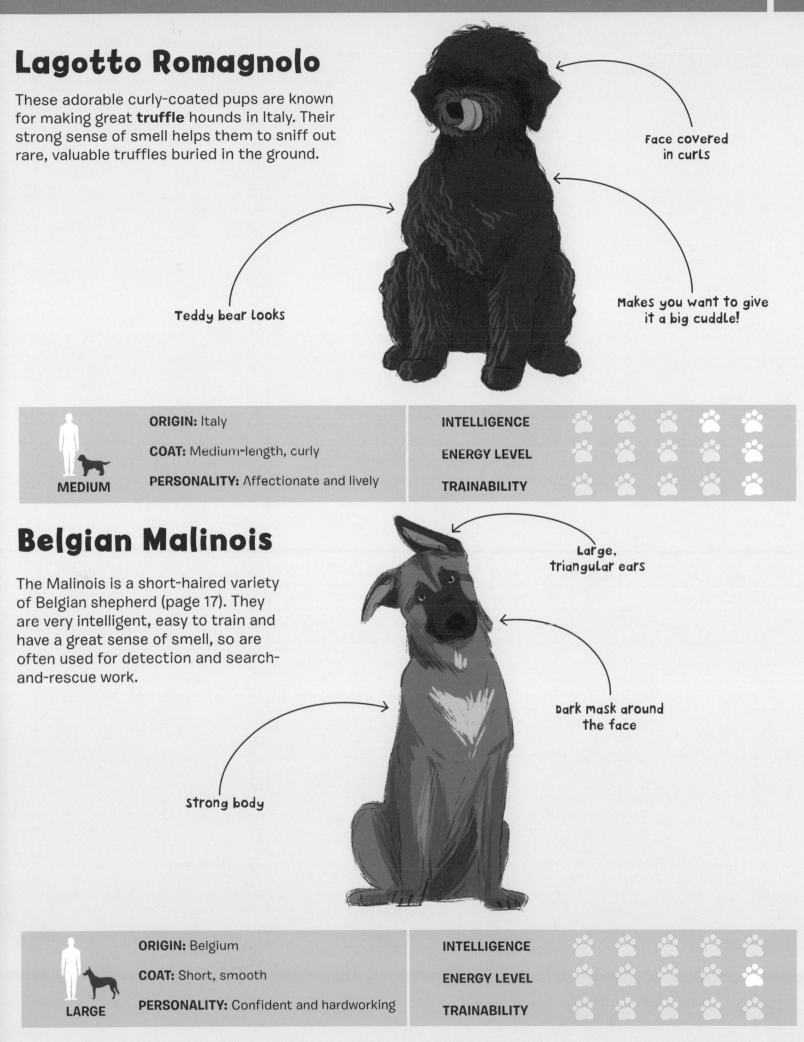

Face covered in curls

Teddy bear looks

Makes you want to give it a big cuddle!

**MEDIUM**

**ORIGIN:** Italy

**COAT:** Medium-length, curly

**PERSONALITY:** Affectionate and lively

INTELLIGENCE

ENERGY LEVEL

TRAINABILITY

# Belgian Malinois

The Malinois is a short-haired variety of Belgian shepherd (page 17). They are very intelligent, easy to train and have a great sense of smell, so are often used for detection and search-and-rescue work.

Large, triangular ears

Dark mask around the face

Strong body

**LARGE**

**ORIGIN:** Belgium

**COAT:** Short, smooth

**PERSONALITY:** Confident and hardworking

INTELLIGENCE

ENERGY LEVEL

TRAINABILITY

# Greyhound

These dogs were born to run! Capable of reaching 45 mph (72 km/h), they win the race for fastest breed in the world.

They are an old breed that were originally bred for hunting, but are now better known as racing dogs.

Long neck

**LARGE**

**ORIGIN:** Belgium

**COAT:** Short, smooth

**PERSONALITY:** Gentle and sensitive

INTELLIGENCE

ENERGY LEVEL

TRAINABILITY

Slim, athletic body

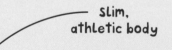

Even though they are super speedy, greyhounds only need short daily bursts of exercise. Afterwards, they will happily spend the rest of their time lounging around and snoozing.

Fantastic eyesight

Long, lanky legs

Long, slim tails

# Saluki

The saluki is one of the world's oldest breeds, with a history dating back thousands of years across the Middle East, from Egypt to Iran. While the greyhound may be a speedier sprinter, the saluki is fastest over long distances. Their top speed is 43 mph (69 km/h).

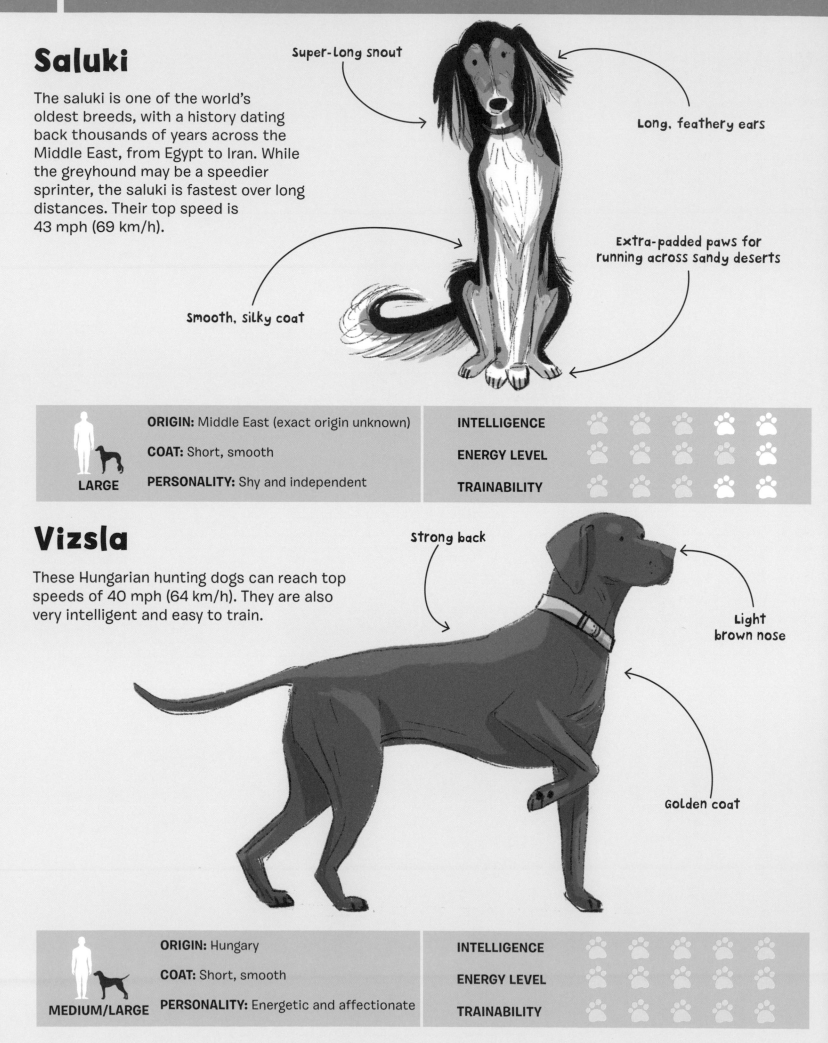

Super-long snout

Long, feathery ears

Extra-padded paws for running across sandy deserts

Smooth, silky coat

**LARGE**

**ORIGIN:** Middle East (exact origin unknown)

**COAT:** Short, smooth

**PERSONALITY:** Shy and independent

| INTELLIGENCE | | | | | |
| ENERGY LEVEL | | | | | |
| TRAINABILITY | | | | | |

# Vizsla

These Hungarian hunting dogs can reach top speeds of 40 mph (64 km/h). They are also very intelligent and easy to train.

Strong back

Light brown nose

Golden coat

**MEDIUM/LARGE**

**ORIGIN:** Hungary

**COAT:** Short, smooth

**PERSONALITY:** Energetic and affectionate

| INTELLIGENCE | | | | | |
| ENERGY LEVEL | | | | | |
| TRAINABILITY | | | | | |

# Whippet

Whippets look a lot like greyhounds (pages 34-35) but are smaller. They're also not quite as speedy, but with a top speed of 35 mph (56 km/h), they are still one of the fastest dogs around!

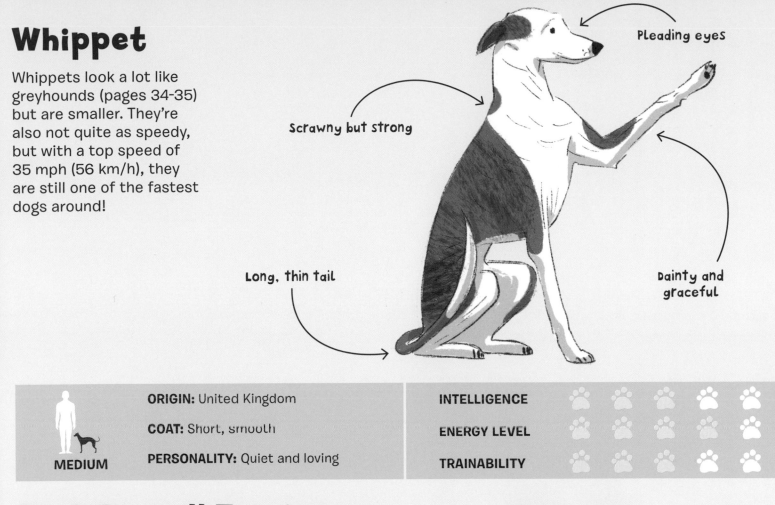

Scrawny but strong

Pleading eyes

Long, thin tail

Dainty and graceful

| MEDIUM | ORIGIN: United Kingdom | | INTELLIGENCE | 🐾 🐾 🐾 🐾 🐾 |
|---|---|---|---|---|
| | COAT: Short, smooth | | ENERGY LEVEL | 🐾 🐾 🐾 🐾 🐾 |
| | PERSONALITY: Quiet and loving | | TRAINABILITY | 🐾 🐾 🐾 🐾 🐾 |

# Jack Russell Terrier

Don't let their little legs fool you. These bouncy little terriers can reach some serious speeds! They are the fastest small breed and can reach speeds of 30 mph (48 km/h).

Loves to play

coats can be smooth or wiry

Small but sturdy

| SMALL | ORIGIN: United Kingdom | | INTELLIGENCE | 🐾 🐾 🐾 🐾 🐾 |
|---|---|---|---|---|
| | COAT: Short, smooth or wiry | | ENERGY LEVEL | 🐾 🐾 🐾 🐾 🐾 |
| | PERSONALITY: Feisty and lively | | TRAINABILITY | 🐾 🐾 🐾 🐾 🐾 |

# Scottish Terrier

"Scotties" were originally bred in the Scottish Highlands. They are quick and feisty little dogs, trained to dig their way into **burrows**. Although, most are now kept as pets, they haven't lost their love for digging!

Upright tail

Bushy eyebrows

Long, thick beard

Short, fluffy legs

**SMALL**

**ORIGIN:** United Kingdom

**COAT:** Medium-length, wiry

**PERSONALITY:** Alert and territorial

| INTELLIGENCE | 🐾 🐾 🐾 🐾 🐾 |
| ENERGY LEVEL | 🐾 🐾 🐾 🐾 🐾 |
| TRAINABILITY | 🐾 🐾 🐾 🐾 🐾 |

# West Highland White Terrier

Most old breeds of terrier were bred to be small enough to fit through tunnels made by burrowing animals. "Westies" are another Scottish breed. They are confident, fun-loving, cuddly little dogs.

Small, pointy ears

Fluffy face

Thick white coat

Short, straight tail

**SMALL**

**ORIGIN:** United Kingdom

**COAT:** Medium-length, thick

**PERSONALITY:** Playful and outgoing

| INTELLIGENCE | 🐾 🐾 🐾 🐾 🐾 |
| ENERGY LEVEL | 🐾 🐾 🐾 🐾 🐾 |
| TRAINABILITY | 🐾 🐾 🐾 🐾 🐾 |

# Border Terrier

Border terriers love to be part of the family. They are good at agility and games. Their hunting instincts are strong, so they may try to chase smaller animals.

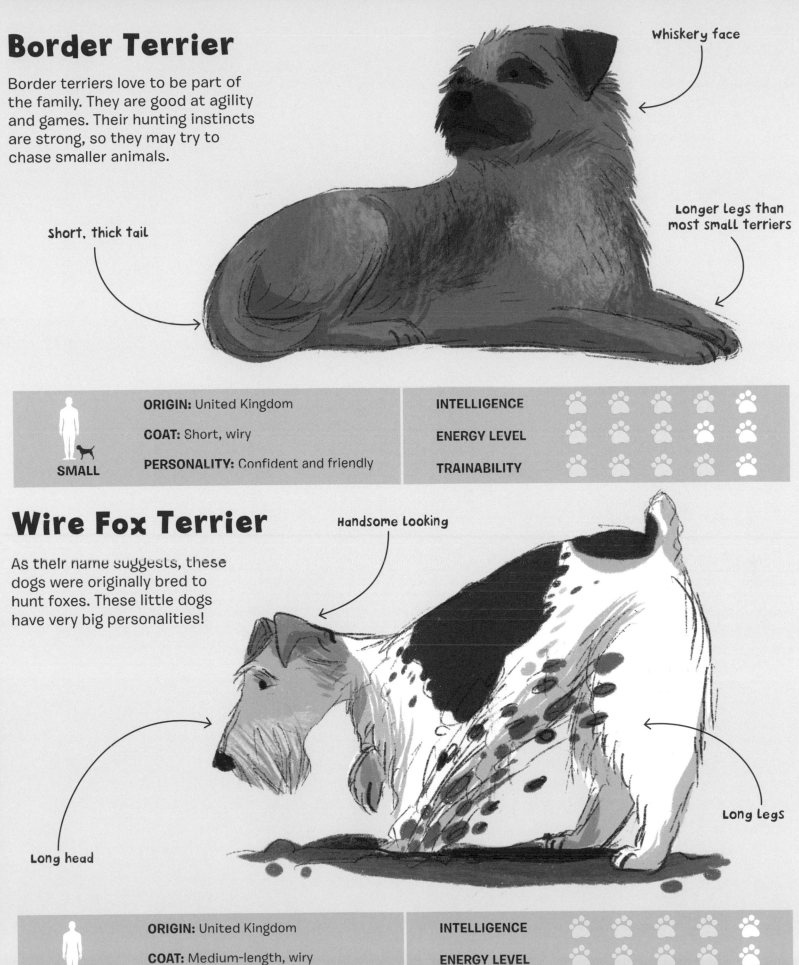

whiskery face

Short, thick tail

Longer legs than most small terriers

**SMALL**

**ORIGIN:** United Kingdom

**COAT:** Short, wiry

**PERSONALITY:** Confident and friendly

INTELLIGENCE

ENERGY LEVEL

TRAINABILITY

# Wire Fox Terrier

Handsome looking

As their name suggests, these dogs were originally bred to hunt foxes. These little dogs have very big personalities!

Long head

Long legs

**SMALL**

**ORIGIN:** United Kingdom

**COAT:** Medium-length, wiry

**PERSONALITY:** Alert and adventurous

INTELLIGENCE

ENERGY LEVEL

TRAINABILITY

# Portuguese Water Dog

These dogs are a fisherman's best friend! Traditionally, they were trained to retrieve fishing equipment from the water, herd fish into nets, and deliver messages between ships. Their "lion cut" hairdo may look weird, but keeping their coats long helped them stay warm in cold waters, while shaving their back legs allowed for easier movement while swimming.

However you style it, their coat needs a lot of grooming!

Feathery tail

Natural swimmers

**MEDIUM**

**ORIGIN:** Portugal

**COAT:** Long, curly/wavy

**PERSONALITY:** Smart and athletic

| | | | | | |
|---|---|---|---|---|---|
| INTELLIGENCE | 🐾 | 🐾 | 🐾 | 🐾 | 🐾 |
| ENERGY LEVEL | 🐾 | 🐾 | 🐾 | 🐾 | 🐾 |
| TRAINABILITY | 🐾 | 🐾 | 🐾 | 🐾 | 🐾 |

# Weimaraner

This striking dog is nicknamed the "Grey Ghost". Graceful, stealthy and energetic, they were bred to be brilliant retrievers, so are fantastic at fetch!

Striking, pale eyes

Shiny silver-grey coat

Stealthy mover

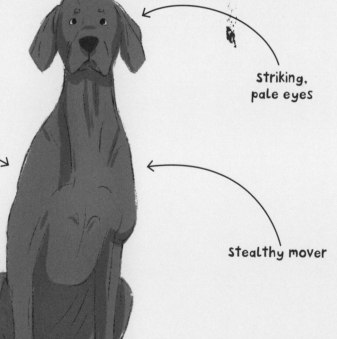

**LARGE**

**ORIGIN:** Germany

**COAT:** Short, smooth

**PERSONALITY:** Active and playful

| | | | | | |
|---|---|---|---|---|---|
| INTELLIGENCE | 🐾 | 🐾 | 🐾 | 🐾 | 🐾 |
| ENERGY LEVEL | 🐾 | 🐾 | 🐾 | 🐾 | 🐾 |
| TRAINABILITY | 🐾 | 🐾 | 🐾 | 🐾 | 🐾 |

# Nova Scotia Duck Tolling Retriever

These dogs are professional fetch players! They were used for an unusual type of hunting, where a hunter would play a game of fetch with their dog to try and lure in curious ducks and geese.

Thick, waterproof coat

Needs a catchier name!

White chest markings

Smallest breed of retriever

**MEDIUM**

**ORIGIN:** Canada

**COAT:** Short, wiry

**PERSONALITY:** Smart and affectionate

INTELLIGENCE

ENERGY LEVEL

TRAINABILITY

# German Pointer

These outdoorsy dogs are brilliant at trailing, tracking and retrieving. They are very energetic and need lots of fresh air and exercise.

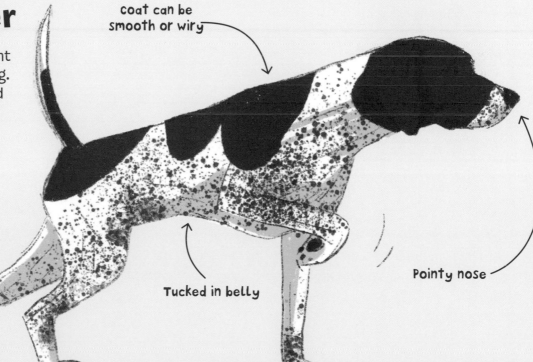

coat can be smooth or wiry

Tucked in belly

Pointy nose

**MEDIUM/LARGE**

**ORIGIN:** Germany

**COAT:** Short, smooth

**PERSONALITY:** Sporty and outgoing

INTELLIGENCE

ENERGY LEVEL

TRAINABILITY

# Treeing Walker Coonhound

This breed is trained to chase raccoons up trees. Some have been known to follow them all the way up the tree! They are energetic and playful dogs, but they can bark a lot.

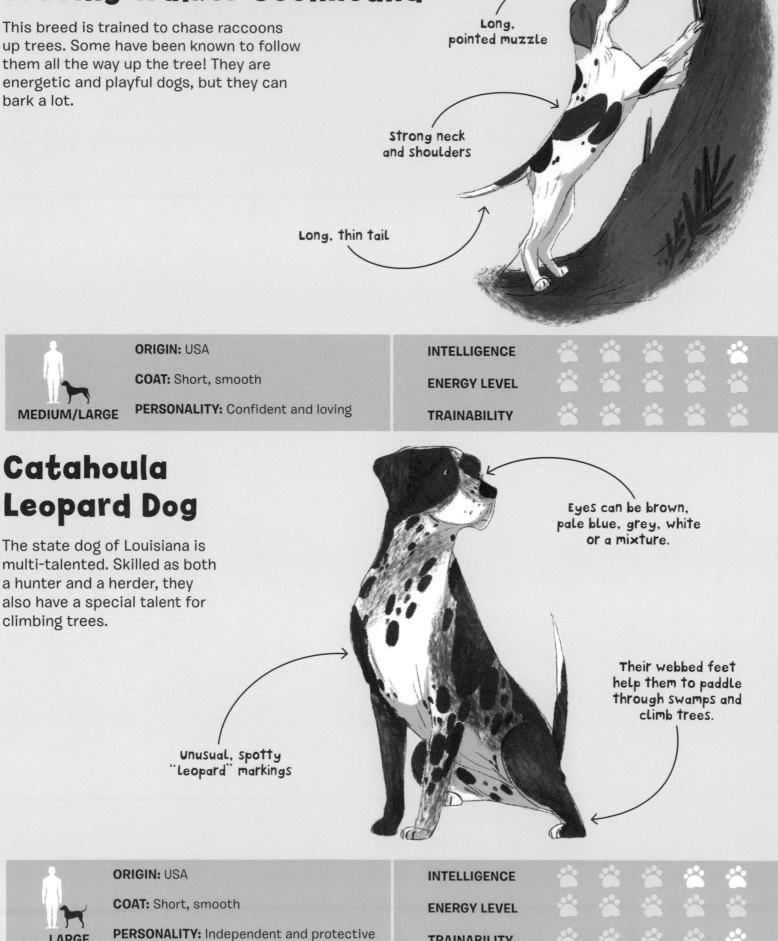

Long, pointed muzzle

Strong neck and shoulders

Long, thin tail

| | ORIGIN: USA | | INTELLIGENCE | 🐾 🐾 🐾 🐾 🐾 |
|---|---|---|---|---|
| | COAT: Short, smooth | | ENERGY LEVEL | 🐾 🐾 🐾 🐾 🐾 |
| MEDIUM/LARGE | PERSONALITY: Confident and loving | | TRAINABILITY | 🐾 🐾 🐾 🐾 🐾 |

# Catahoula Leopard Dog

The state dog of Louisiana is multi-talented. Skilled as both a hunter and a herder, they also have a special talent for climbing trees.

Eyes can be brown, pale blue, grey, white or a mixture.

Their webbed feet help them to paddle through swamps and climb trees.

Unusual, spotty "Leopard" markings

| | ORIGIN: USA | | INTELLIGENCE | 🐾 🐾 🐾 🐾 🐾 |
|---|---|---|---|---|
| | COAT: Short, smooth | | ENERGY LEVEL | 🐾 🐾 🐾 🐾 🐾 |
| LARGE | PERSONALITY: Independent and protective | | TRAINABILITY | 🐾 🐾 🐾 🐾 🐾 |

# Norwegian Lundehund

One of the rarest dogs in the world, the Norwegian lundehund was once used to hunt **puffins**. They would have to climb difficult and dangerous cliffs, in search of nests. Thanks to some very unusual physical features, these dogs make incredible rock climbers.

"Elastic" neck can bend all the way back to touch the spine

An extra toe on each foot to help grip rocks

SMALL

**ORIGIN:** Norway

**COAT:** Short, thick

**PERSONALITY:** Alert and cheerful

INTELLIGENCE

ENERGY LEVEL

TRAINABILITY

Ears can fold shut to protect from dirt and pests

Flexible front legs can stretch all the way out from the body

# CUDDLY COMPANIONS

It is often said that dogs are "man's best friend". They can be loving, loyal and funny companions. Some dogs are able to provide their owners with emotional and physical support too. From fluffy little lapdogs to supportive service dogs, the dogs in this section all make fantastic human companions.

# Pug

These popular pups have a long history as **lapdogs**. They were the valued companions of ancient Chinese emperors, and became popular among wealthy Europeans from the 16th century. Their squished faces often lead to difficulty breathing, and other health problems.

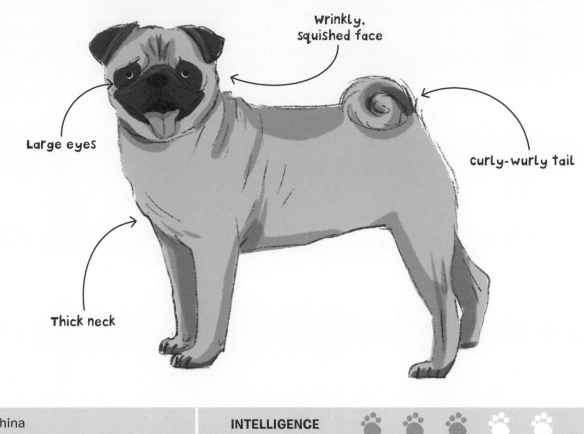

wrinkly, squished face

Large eyes

curly-wurly tail

Thick neck

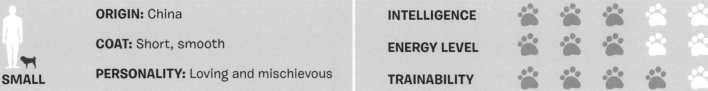

**SMALL**

**ORIGIN:** China

**COAT:** Short, smooth

**PERSONALITY:** Loving and mischievous

| INTELLIGENCE | 🐾 | 🐾 | 🐾 | | |
| ENERGY LEVEL | 🐾 | 🐾 | 🐾 | | |
| TRAINABILITY | 🐾 | 🐾 | 🐾 | 🐾 | |

# Papillion

This tiny breed can be easily identified by its large feathery ears. Papillions appear on the laps of royalty in many old European paintings. They are affectionate dogs who love to play.

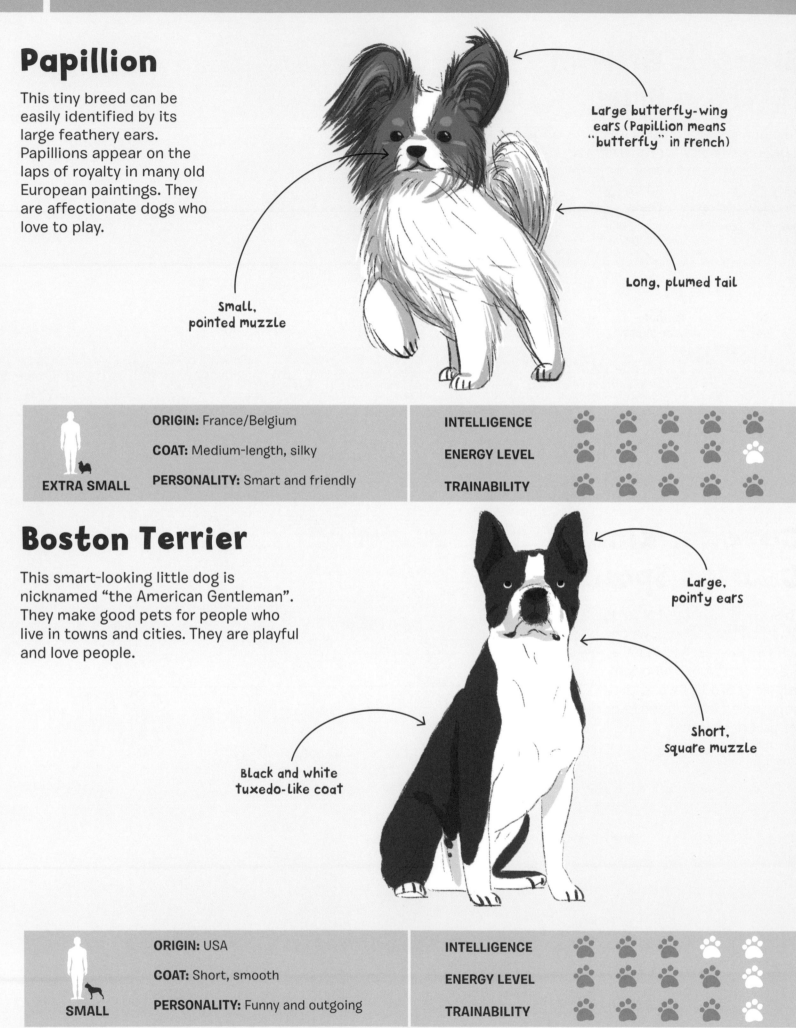

Large butterfly-wing ears (Papillion means "butterfly" in French)

Long, plumed tail

Small, pointed muzzle

| | | INTELLIGENCE | 🐾 🐾 🐾 🐾 🐾 |
|---|---|---|---|
| | **ORIGIN:** France/Belgium | | |
| | **COAT:** Medium-length, silky | ENERGY LEVEL | 🐾 🐾 🐾 🐾 🐾 |
| **EXTRA SMALL** | **PERSONALITY:** Smart and friendly | TRAINABILITY | 🐾 🐾 🐾 🐾 🐾 |

# Boston Terrier

This smart-looking little dog is nicknamed "the American Gentleman". They make good pets for people who live in towns and cities. They are playful and love people.

Large, pointy ears

Short, square muzzle

Black and white tuxedo-like coat

| | | INTELLIGENCE | 🐾 🐾 🐾 🐾 🐾 |
|---|---|---|---|
| | **ORIGIN:** USA | | |
| | **COAT:** Short, smooth | ENERGY LEVEL | 🐾 🐾 🐾 🐾 🐾 |
| **SMALL** | **PERSONALITY:** Funny and outgoing | TRAINABILITY | 🐾 🐾 🐾 🐾 🐾 |

# Brussels Griffon (Griffon Bruxellois)

This unusual toy breed (see page 11) has a big personality for its size! They are playful and easy to train. They love to be part of the family and can get lonely when left on their own for too long.

Bearded face

Short muzzle

coats can be medium-length and wiry or short and smooth

| | | | | | | |
|---|---|---|---|---|---|---|
|  **EXTRA SMALL** | **ORIGIN:** Belgium | | **INTELLIGENCE** | 🐾🐾🐾 | | |
| | **COAT:** Medium length, wiry | | **ENERGY LEVEL** | 🐾🐾🐾 | | |
| | **PERSONALITY:** Loyal and playful | | **TRAINABILITY** | 🐾🐾🐾🐾 | | |

# Cavalier King Charles Spaniel

This breed is named after King Charles II of England, who kept similar dogs. Unlike most other breeds of spaniel, who were originally bred to work, these dogs have always been kept purely for companionship.

Long, fluffy ears

Silky coat

Feathery legs

| | | | | | | |
|---|---|---|---|---|---|---|
| **SMALL** | **ORIGIN:** United Kingdom | | **INTELLIGENCE** | 🐾🐾🐾 | | |
| | **COAT:** Medium-length, wavy, silky | | **ENERGY LEVEL** | 🐾🐾🐾 | | |
| | **PERSONALITY:** Gentle and affectionate | | **TRAINABILITY** | 🐾🐾🐾🐾 | | |

# French Bulldog

This mini bulldog breed is a popular pet. They are particularly good for people who live in small apartments, as they don't need a lot of outdoor exercise. They also make handy watchdogs, as they are always alert.

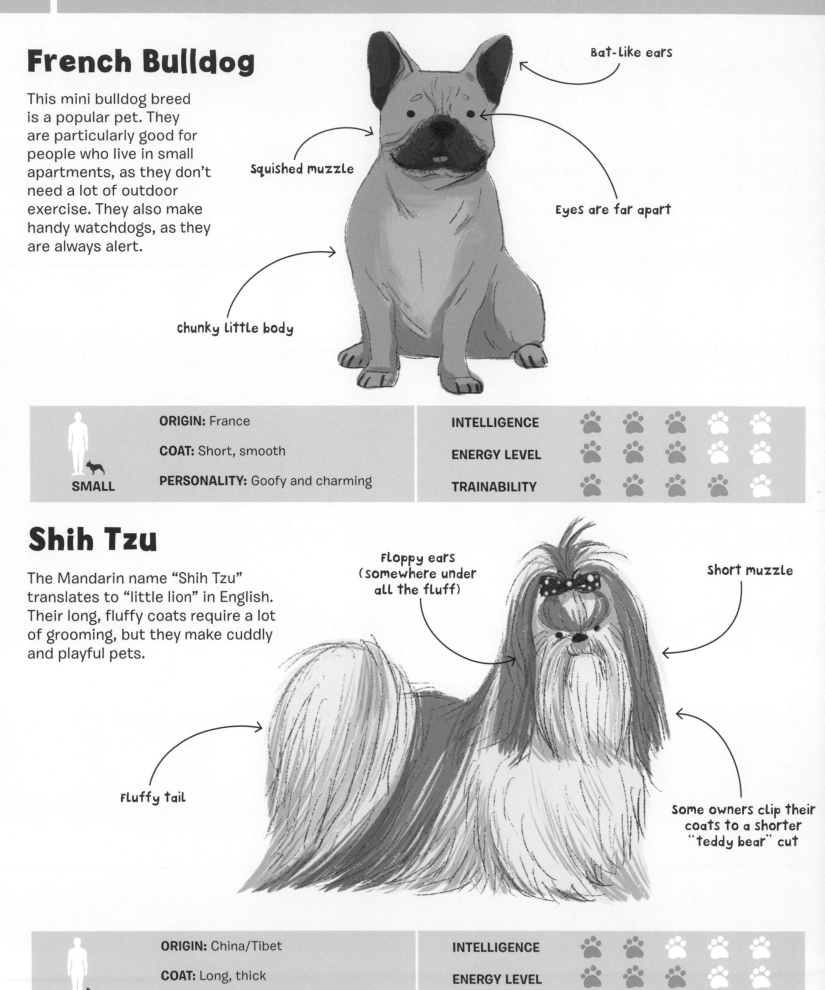

Bat-like ears

Squished muzzle

Eyes are far apart

chunky little body

| | | INTELLIGENCE | 🐾 🐾 🐾 🐾 🐾 |
|---|---|---|---|
| **SMALL** | **ORIGIN:** France | ENERGY LEVEL | 🐾 🐾 🐾 🐾 🐾 |
| | **COAT:** Short, smooth | TRAINABILITY | 🐾 🐾 🐾 🐾 🐾 |
| | **PERSONALITY:** Goofy and charming | | |

# Shih Tzu

The Mandarin name "Shih Tzu" translates to "little lion" in English. Their long, fluffy coats require a lot of grooming, but they make cuddly and playful pets.

Floppy ears (somewhere under all the fluff)

Short muzzle

Fluffy tail

Some owners clip their coats to a shorter "teddy bear" cut

| | | INTELLIGENCE | 🐾 🐾 🐾 🐾 🐾 |
|---|---|---|---|
| **EXTRA SMALL** | **ORIGIN:** China/Tibet | ENERGY LEVEL | 🐾 🐾 🐾 🐾 🐾 |
| | **COAT:** Long, thick | TRAINABILITY | 🐾 🐾 🐾 🐾 🐾 |
| | **PERSONALITY:** Playful and affectionate | | |

# Bolognese

These scruffy little dogs are real couch potatoes that don't require a lot of exercise. They love being with people and don't like to be left alone for long.

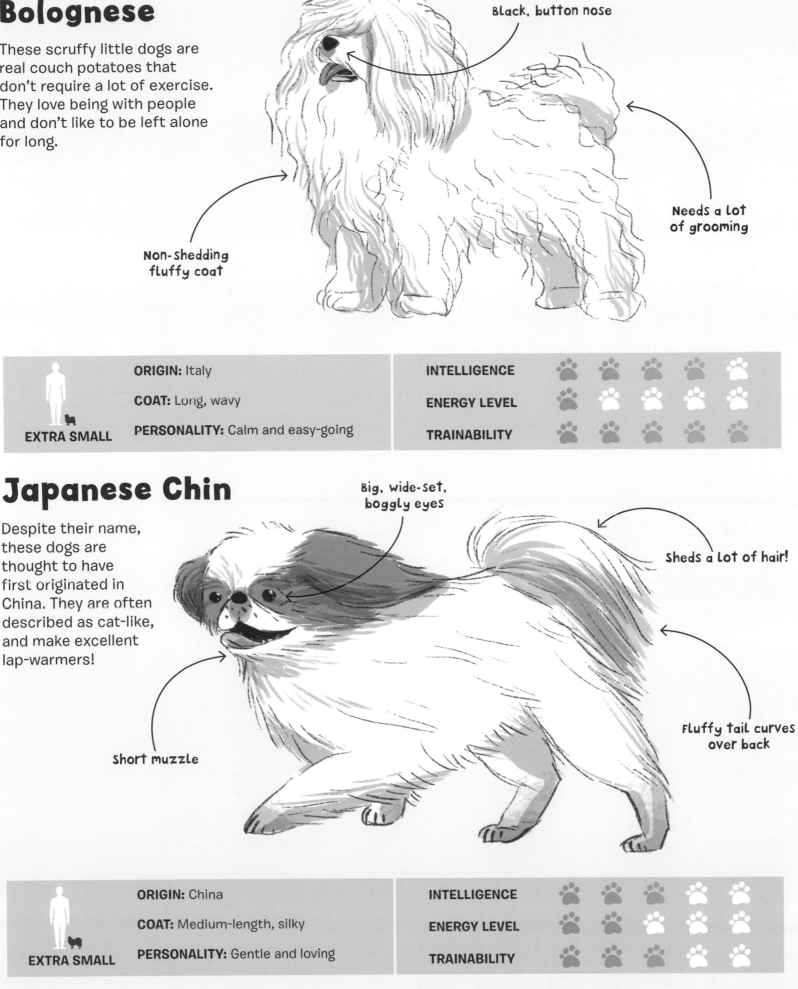

Black, button nose

Needs a lot of grooming

Non-shedding fluffy coat

| | | INTELLIGENCE | 🐾 🐾 🐾 🐾 🐾 |
|---|---|---|---|
| **EXTRA SMALL** | **ORIGIN:** Italy | ENERGY LEVEL | 🐾 🐾 🐾 🐾 🐾 |
| | **COAT:** Long, wavy | TRAINABILITY | 🐾 🐾 🐾 🐾 🐾 |
| | **PERSONALITY:** Calm and easy-going | | |

# Japanese Chin

Despite their name, these dogs are thought to have first originated in China. They are often described as cat-like, and make excellent lap-warmers!

Big, wide-set, boggly eyes

Sheds a lot of hair!

Short muzzle

Fluffy tail curves over back

| | | INTELLIGENCE | 🐾 🐾 🐾 🐾 🐾 |
|---|---|---|---|
| **EXTRA SMALL** | **ORIGIN:** China | ENERGY LEVEL | 🐾 🐾 🐾 🐾 🐾 |
| | **COAT:** Medium-length, silky | TRAINABILITY | 🐾 🐾 🐾 🐾 🐾 |
| | **PERSONALITY:** Gentle and loving | | |

# Toy Poodle

The smallest of four different sizes of the popular poodle (page 71), reaching a maximum of 10 inches (25 cm) tall. They may be tiny, but they are just as smart and athletic as their larger brothers and sisters.

Thick, curly coat

Can be clipped and groomed in different styles

Weighing under 6 pounds (2.7kg)

| | | INTELLIGENCE | 🐾 🐾 🐾 🐾 🐾 |
|---|---|---|---|
| | **ORIGIN:** Germany | | |
| | **COAT:** Long, curly | ENERGY LEVEL | 🐾 🐾 🐾 🐾 🐾 |
| **EXTRA SMALL** | **PERSONALITY:** Smart and confident | TRAINABILITY | 🐾 🐾 🐾 🐾 🐾 |

# Miniature Pinscher

Also known as "Min Pins", these dogs are a mini breed of pinscher that look similar to the larger Dobermanns (Doberman pinscher (page 26). They were originally used as farmyard rat-hunters.

Straight back

Upright tail

Shiny, black and tan coat

| | | INTELLIGENCE | 🐾 🐾 🐾 🐾 🐾 |
|---|---|---|---|
| | **ORIGIN:** Germany | | |
| | **COAT:** Short, smooth | ENERGY LEVEL | 🐾 🐾 🐾 🐾 🐾 |
| **EXTRA SMALL** | **PERSONALITY:** Fearless and outgoing | TRAINABILITY | 🐾 🐾 🐾 🐾 🐾 |

# Alaskan Klee Kai

This miniature husky-type dog comes in three sizes, with a height range of 12–17 inches (30–44 cm). They look similar to the much larger Siberian husky (page 20) and Alaskan malamute (page 22), but were bred as house dogs, rather than to pull sleds.

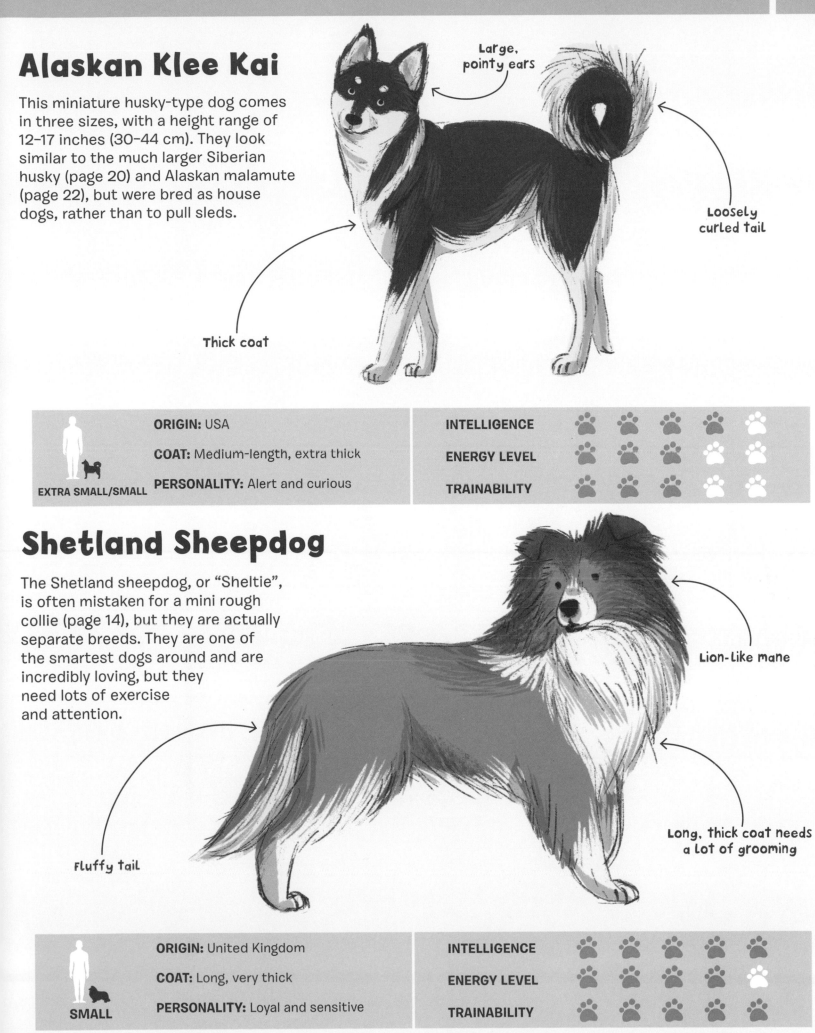

Large, pointy ears

Loosely curled tail

Thick coat

| | | INTELLIGENCE | 🐾 🐾 🐾 🐾 🐾 |
|---|---|---|---|
| **EXTRA SMALL/SMALL** | **ORIGIN:** USA | ENERGY LEVEL | 🐾 🐾 🐾 🐾 🐾 |
| | **COAT:** Medium-length, extra thick | TRAINABILITY | 🐾 🐾 🐾 🐾 🐾 |
| | **PERSONALITY:** Alert and curious | | |

# Shetland Sheepdog

The Shetland sheepdog, or "Sheltie", is often mistaken for a mini rough collie (page 14), but they are actually separate breeds. They are one of the smartest dogs around and are incredibly loving, but they need lots of exercise and attention.

Lion-like mane

Long, thick coat needs a lot of grooming

Fluffy tail

| | | INTELLIGENCE | 🐾 🐾 🐾 🐾 🐾 |
|---|---|---|---|
| **SMALL** | **ORIGIN:** United Kingdom | ENERGY LEVEL | 🐾 🐾 🐾 🐾 🐾 |
| | **COAT:** Long, very thick | TRAINABILITY | 🐾 🐾 🐾 🐾 🐾 |
| | **PERSONALITY:** Loyal and sensitive | | |

# HEROIC HELPERS

Service or assistance dogs are trained to help people with disabilities. This includes guide dogs for the blind and visually impaired, hearing dogs to assist deaf and hard-of-hearing people, mobility service dogs to help people with physical disabilities, and medical-response dogs to help people manage medical conditions.

A service dog's duties can include helping people move around, completing household tasks, providing medical assistance, and offering emotional support and company. Lots of different breeds are used as service dogs, but some are particularly popular.

Guide dog for the blind

# Labrador Retriever

Labs have long been the most popular dog in the USA, the UK and many other countries around the world. They are loving, highly intelligent, steady and reliable, all of which are great qualities for guide dogs for the blind and for other service and assistance work.

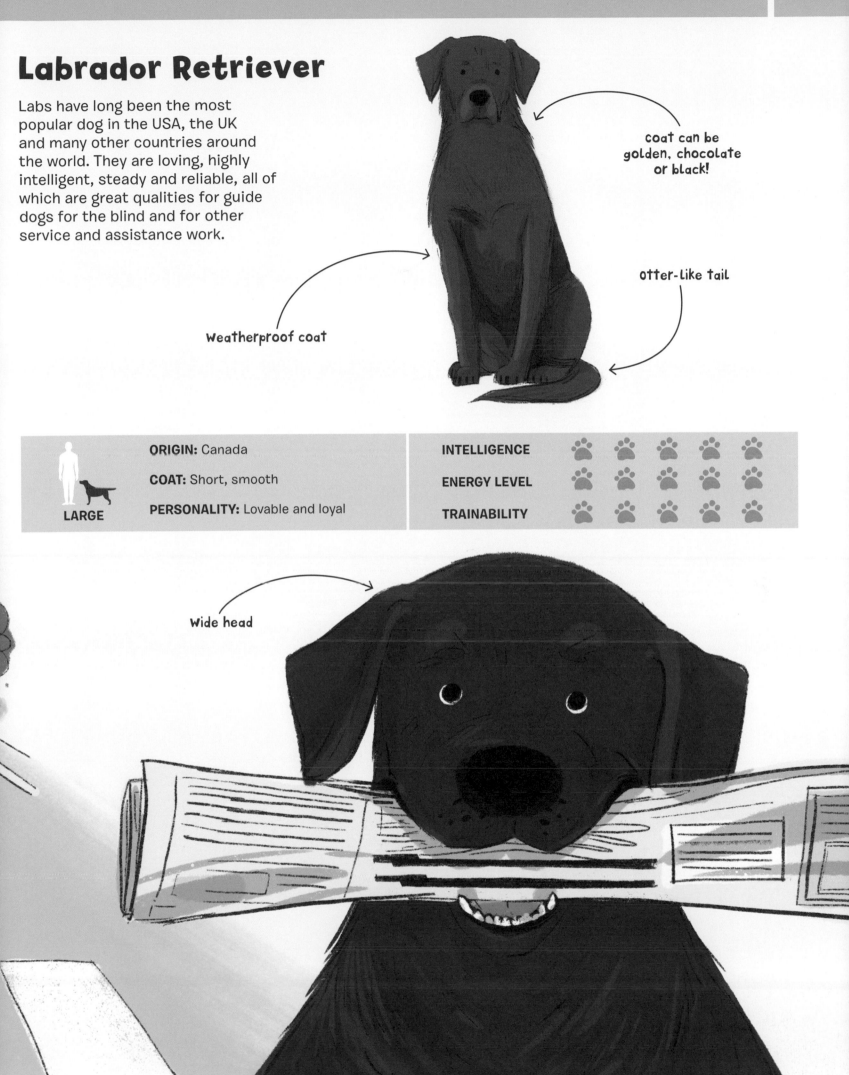

coat can be golden, chocolate or black!

otter-like tail

Weatherproof coat

**ORIGIN:** Canada

**COAT:** Short, smooth

**PERSONALITY:** Lovable and loyal

LARGE

INTELLIGENCE

ENERGY LEVEL

TRAINABILITY

Wide head

# Golden Retriever

Golden retrievers are big people-pleasers, that makes them affectionate family pets and also smart working dogs.

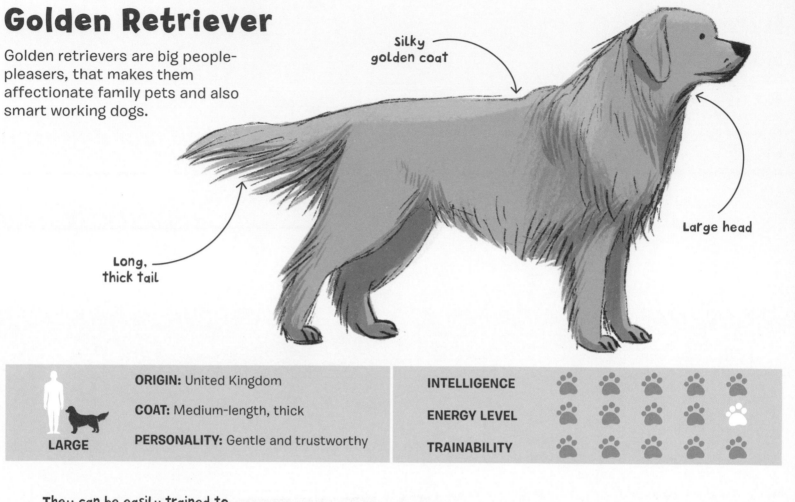

Silky golden coat

Large head

Long, thick tail

**LARGE**

**ORIGIN:** United Kingdom

**COAT:** Medium-length, thick

**PERSONALITY:** Gentle and trustworthy

INTELLIGENCE 🐾🐾🐾🐾🐾

ENERGY LEVEL 🐾🐾🐾🐾🐾

TRAINABILITY 🐾🐾🐾🐾🐾

They can be easily trained to perform many different tasks, including laundry!

# Irish Setter

Often known simply as "red setters" because of their distinctive auburn coat. Their sweet, affectionate, and sociable personalities have made them popular as **therapy dogs**, to be taken into schools, hospitals and nursing homes.

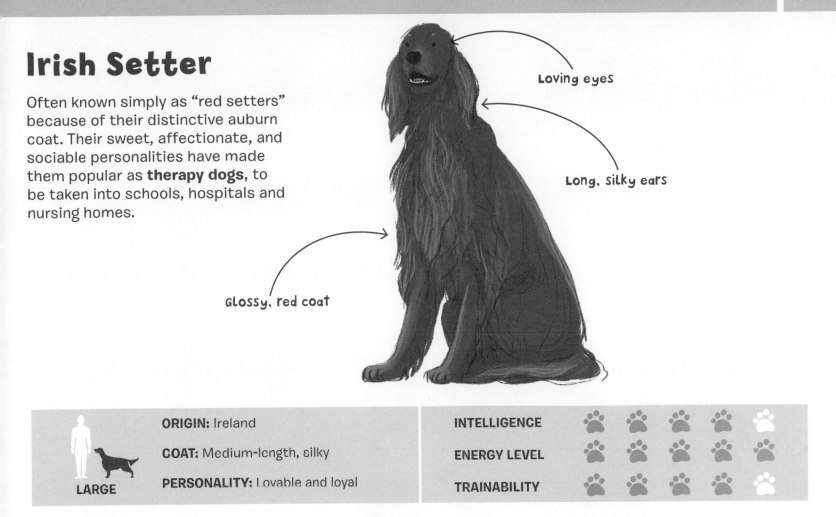

Loving eyes

Long, silky ears

Glossy, red coat

LARGE

**ORIGIN:** Ireland

**COAT:** Medium-length, silky

**PERSONALITY:** Lovable and loyal

| INTELLIGENCE | 🐾 🐾 🐾 🐾 🐾 |
| --- | --- |
| ENERGY LEVEL | 🐾 🐾 🐾 🐾 🐾 |
| TRAINABILITY | 🐾 🐾 🐾 🐾 🐾 |

# Pomeranian

Service dogs don't have to be big! Aside from being adorable balls of fluff, Pomeranians are highly intelligent and loving. They make great emotional-support dogs, medical-response dogs and can also assist people who have difficulties hearing or have no hearing at all.

Fluffy coat

Super soft and fluffy

Foxy face

EXTRA SMALL

**ORIGIN:** Germany

**COAT:** Long, very thick

**PERSONALITY:** Friendly and smart

| INTELLIGENCE | 🐾 🐾 🐾 🐾 🐾 |
| --- | --- |
| ENERGY LEVEL | 🐾 🐾 🐾 🐾 🐾 |
| TRAINABILITY | 🐾 🐾 🐾 🐾 🐾 |

# Shiba Inu

This ancient breed has been much loved in its homeland of Japan for centuries, and has recently been gaining popularity across the rest of the world.

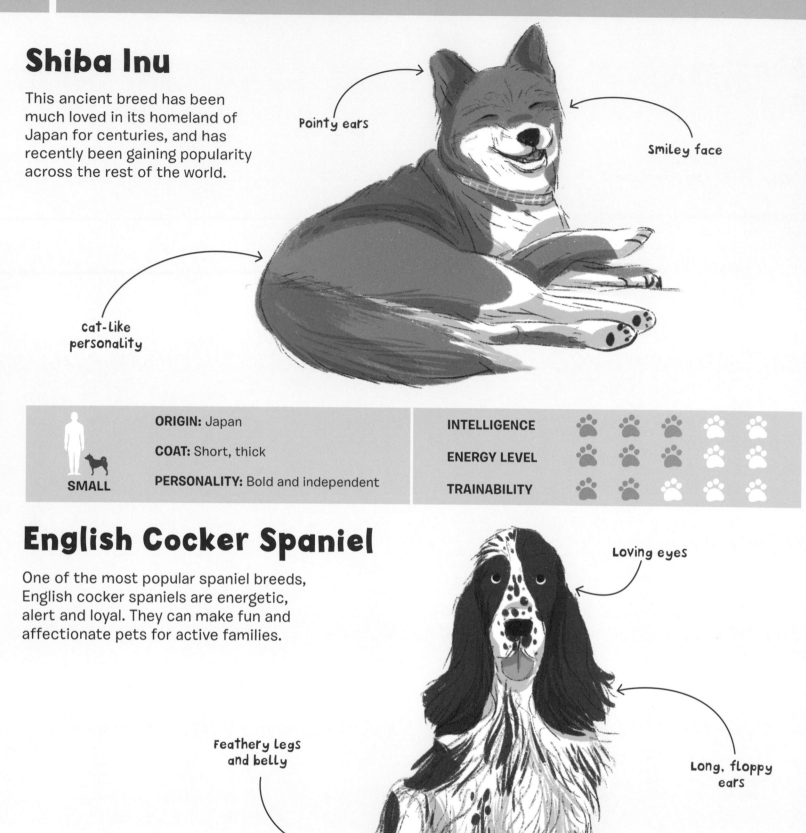

Pointy ears

Smiley face

cat-like personality

| | | |
|---|---|---|
| SMALL | **ORIGIN:** Japan | |
| | **COAT:** Short, thick | |
| | **PERSONALITY:** Bold and independent | |

| | |
|---|---|
| INTELLIGENCE | 🐾🐾🐾🐾🐾 |
| ENERGY LEVEL | 🐾🐾🐾🐾🐾 |
| TRAINABILITY | 🐾🐾🐾🐾🐾 |

# English Cocker Spaniel

One of the most popular spaniel breeds, English cocker spaniels are energetic, alert and loyal. They can make fun and affectionate pets for active families.

Loving eyes

Feathery legs and belly

Long, floppy ears

| | | |
|---|---|---|
| MEDIUM | **ORIGIN:** United Kingdom | |
| | **COAT:** Medium-length/long, wavy | |
| | **PERSONALITY:** Friendly and outgoing | |

| | |
|---|---|
| INTELLIGENCE | 🐾🐾🐾🐾🐾 |
| ENERGY LEVEL | 🐾🐾🐾🐾🐾 |
| TRAINABILITY | 🐾🐾🐾🐾🐾 |

# Staffordshire Bull Terrier

"Staffies" often have a bad reputation because of their history as fighting dogs, but they are actually some of the sweetest, most affectionate dogs you will ever meet!

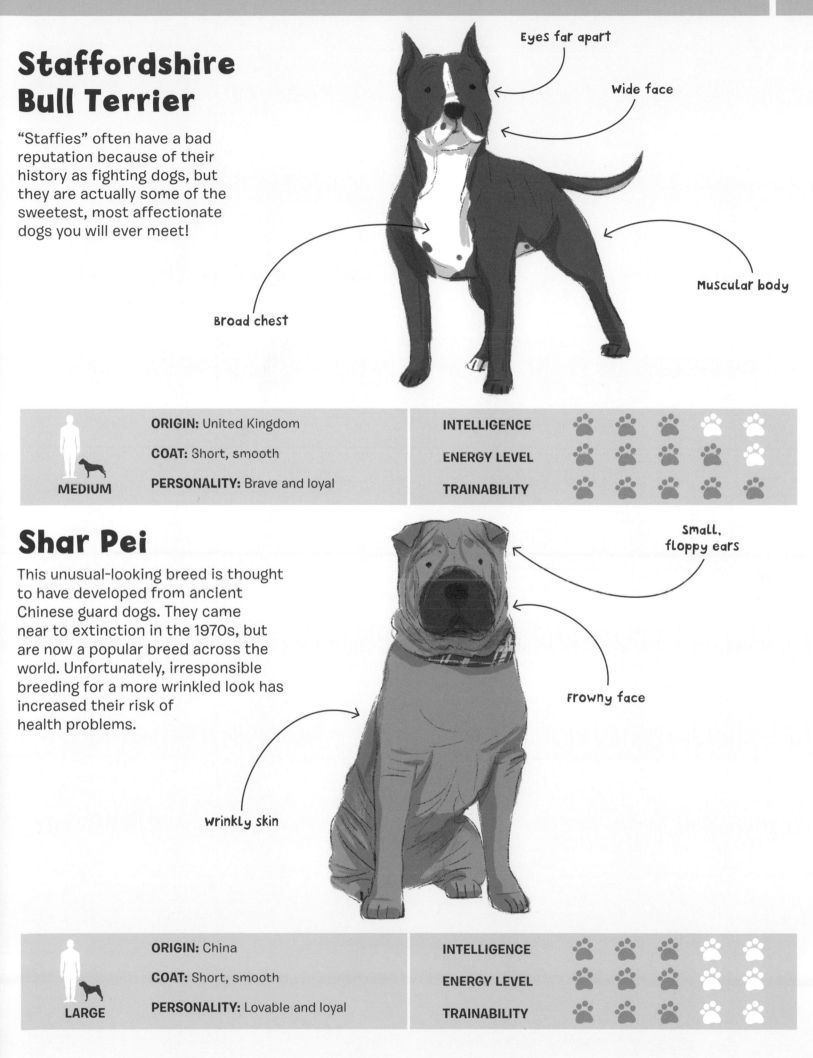

Eyes far apart

Wide face

Muscular body

Broad chest

| | | |
|---|---|---|
| **ORIGIN:** United Kingdom | **INTELLIGENCE** | 🐾 🐾 🐾 🐾 🐾 |
| **COAT:** Short, smooth | **ENERGY LEVEL** | 🐾 🐾 🐾 🐾 🐾 |
| MEDIUM — **PERSONALITY:** Brave and loyal | **TRAINABILITY** | 🐾 🐾 🐾 🐾 🐾 |

# Shar Pei

This unusual-looking breed is thought to have developed from ancient Chinese guard dogs. They came near to extinction in the 1970s, but are now a popular breed across the world. Unfortunately, irresponsible breeding for a more wrinkled look has increased their risk of health problems.

Small, floppy ears

Frowny face

Wrinkly skin

| | | |
|---|---|---|
| **ORIGIN:** China | **INTELLIGENCE** | 🐾 🐾 🐾 🐾 🐾 |
| **COAT:** Short, smooth | **ENERGY LEVEL** | 🐾 🐾 🐾 🐾 🐾 |
| LARGE — **PERSONALITY:** Lovable and loyal | **TRAINABILITY** | 🐾 🐾 🐾 🐾 🐾 |

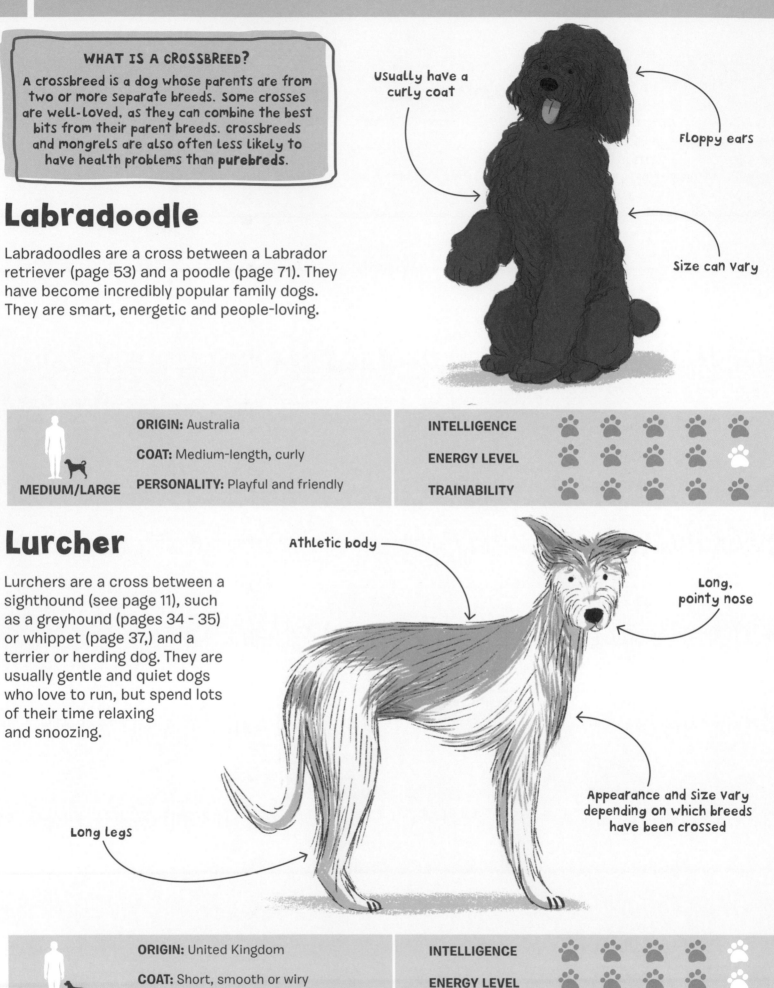

**WHAT IS A CROSSBREED?**
A crossbreed is a dog whose parents are from two or more separate breeds. Some crosses are well-loved, as they can combine the best bits from their parent breeds. crossbreeds and mongrels are also often less likely to have health problems than **purebreds**.

Usually have a curly coat

Floppy ears

Size can vary

# Labradoodle

Labradoodles are a cross between a Labrador retriever (page 53) and a poodle (page 71). They have become incredibly popular family dogs. They are smart, energetic and people-loving.

**ORIGIN:** Australia

**COAT:** Medium-length, curly

**PERSONALITY:** Playful and friendly

**MEDIUM/LARGE**

INTELLIGENCE

ENERGY LEVEL

TRAINABILITY

# Lurcher

Athletic body

Long, pointy nose

Lurchers are a cross between a sighthound (see page 11), such as a greyhound (pages 34 - 35) or whippet (page 37,) and a terrier or herding dog. They are usually gentle and quiet dogs who love to run, but spend lots of their time relaxing and snoozing.

Appearance and size vary depending on which breeds have been crossed

Long legs

**ORIGIN:** United Kingdom

**COAT:** Short, smooth or wiry

**PERSONALITY:** Peaceful and loving

**MEDIUM/LARGE**

INTELLIGENCE

ENERGY LEVEL

TRAINABILITY

# Puggle

A puggle is a cross between a pug (page 45) and a beagle (page 32). They are taller and more energetic than a pug, and are less likely to have health issues.

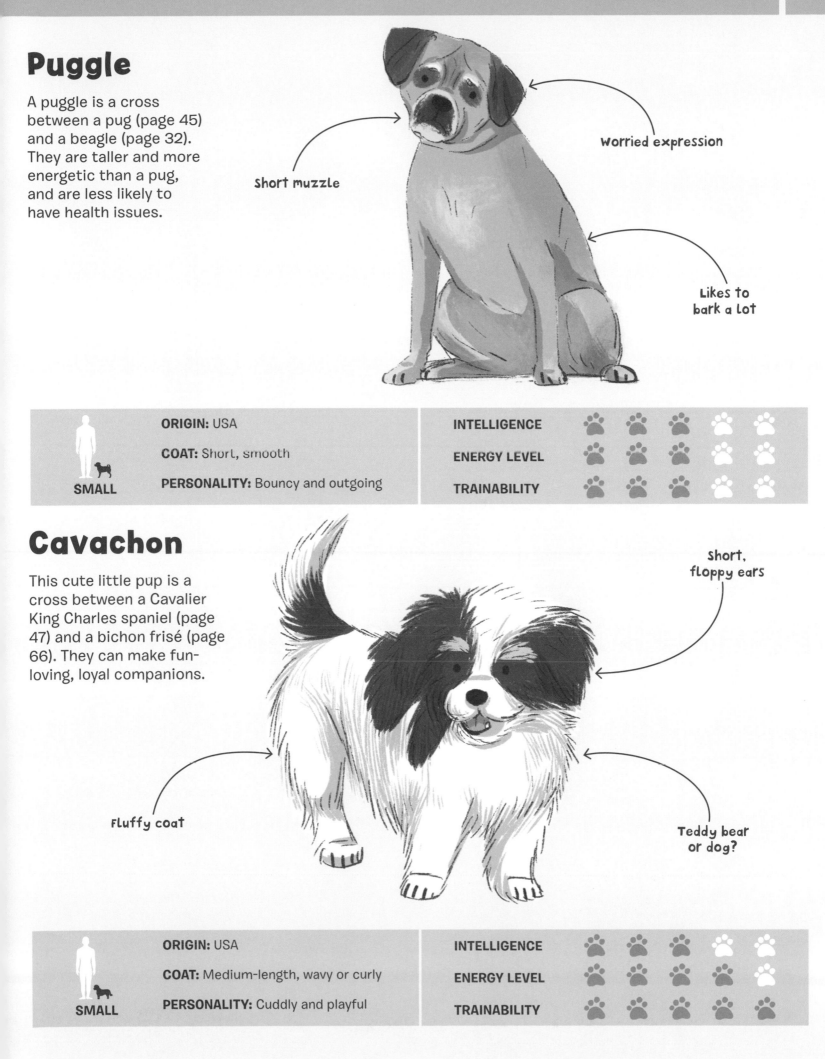

Short muzzle

Worried expression

Likes to bark a lot

| | | | | | | |
|---|---|---|---|---|---|---|
| **SMALL** | **ORIGIN:** USA | | INTELLIGENCE | 🐾 🐾 🐾 ⚪ ⚪ | | |
| | **COAT:** Short, smooth | | ENERGY LEVEL | 🐾 🐾 🐾 🐾 ⚪ | | |
| | **PERSONALITY:** Bouncy and outgoing | | TRAINABILITY | 🐾 🐾 🐾 ⚪ ⚪ | | |

# Cavachon

This cute little pup is a cross between a Cavalier King Charles spaniel (page 47) and a bichon frisé (page 66). They can make fun-loving, loyal companions.

Short, floppy ears

Fluffy coat

Teddy bear or dog?

| | | | | | | |
|---|---|---|---|---|---|---|
| **SMALL** | **ORIGIN:** USA | | INTELLIGENCE | 🐾 🐾 🐾 ⚪ ⚪ | | |
| | **COAT:** Medium-length, wavy or curly | | ENERGY LEVEL | 🐾 🐾 🐾 🐾 ⚪ | | |
| | **PERSONALITY:** Cuddly and playful | | TRAINABILITY | 🐾 🐾 🐾 🐾 🐾 | | |

# PAWSOME PUP AWARDS

Welcome to the Pawsome Pup Awards!
We're celebrating dogs who dare to be
different. From the biggest to the smallest,
the fluffiest to the spottiest, these dogs all
have something that makes them stand out
from the crowd. Dotty Dalmatians, popular
poodles, and the rare yodelling New Guinea
singing dog all feature on the list of amazing
award winners. Which dog would you honour
with the award for funniest hairdo?

# Irish Wolfhound

The award for the tallest dog goes to the Irish wolfhound. This shaggy dog can reach a whopping 34 inches (86 cm) in height and weighs up to 150 pounds (68 kg). They are gentle giants who love spending time with their humans.

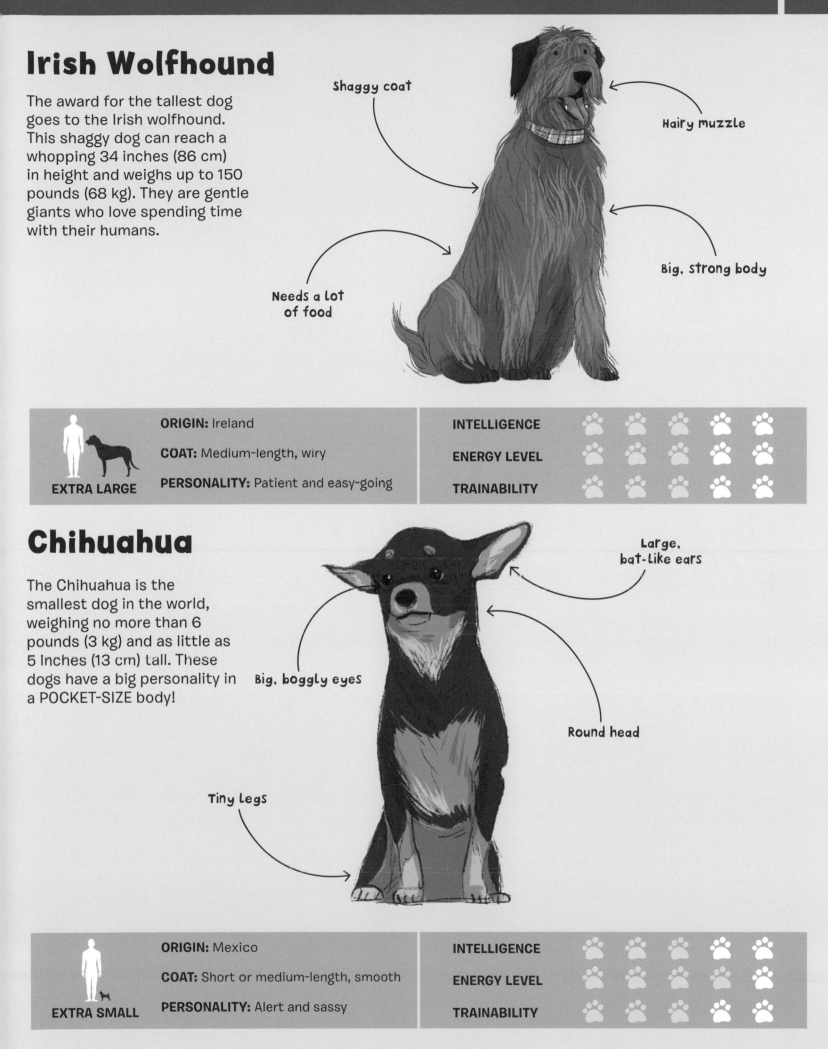

Shaggy coat

Hairy muzzle

Big, strong body

Needs a lot of food

**ORIGIN:** Ireland

**COAT:** Medium-length, wiry

**PERSONALITY:** Patient and easy-going

EXTRA LARGE

INTELLIGENCE

ENERGY LEVEL

TRAINABILITY

# Chihuahua

The Chihuahua is the smallest dog in the world, weighing no more than 6 pounds (3 kg) and as little as 5 Inches (13 cm) tall. These dogs have a big personality in a POCKET-SIZE body!

Large, bat-like ears

Big, boggly eyes

Round head

Tiny legs

**ORIGIN:** Mexico

**COAT:** Short or medium-length, smooth

**PERSONALITY:** Alert and sassy

EXTRA SMALL

INTELLIGENCE

ENERGY LEVEL

TRAINABILITY

# Bulldog

Bulldogs are well known for their short, upturned noses. This famous breed is known for being brave and friendly, but they can also be quite stubborn.

chunky body

Grumpy old man face

Big **underbite**

Waddling walk

| | | |
|---|---|---|
| **MEDIUM** | **ORIGIN:** United Kingdom | **INTELLIGENCE** |
| | **COAT:** Short, smooth | **ENERGY LEVEL** |
| | **PERSONALITY:** Sweet and goofy | **TRAINABILITY** |

# Affenpinscher

Affenpinschers have monkey-like looks, with a flat face and tiny nose with wide nostrils. These little dogs are confident, curious and funny.

Round, hairy face

Upright tail

Tiny nose with wide nostrils

Black, wiry coat

| | | |
|---|---|---|
| **EXTRA SMALL** | **ORIGIN:** Germany | **INTELLIGENCE** |
| | **COAT:** Medium-length, wiry | **ENERGY LEVEL** |
| | **PERSONALITY:** Mischievous and stubborn | **TRAINABILITY** |

# Bull Terrier

Bull terriers are famous for their long "egg heads", and sloping noses. They are playful and clownish characters with bundles of confidence.

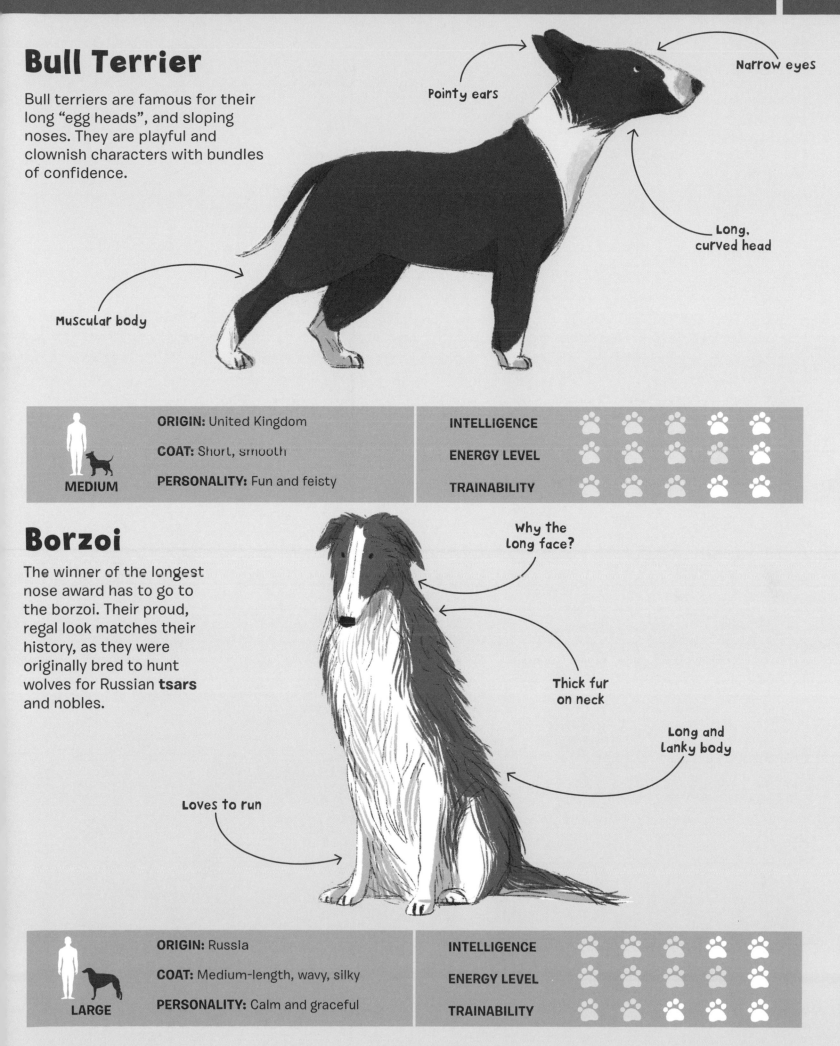

Pointy ears

Narrow eyes

Long, curved head

Muscular body

| | ORIGIN: United Kingdom | INTELLIGENCE | 🐾 🐾 🐾 🐾 🐾 |
| --- | --- | --- | --- |
| | COAT: Short, smooth | ENERGY LEVEL | 🐾 🐾 🐾 🐾 🐾 |
| MEDIUM | PERSONALITY: Fun and feisty | TRAINABILITY | 🐾 🐾 🐾 🐾 🐾 |

# Borzoi

The winner of the longest nose award has to go to the borzoi. Their proud, regal look matches their history, as they were originally bred to hunt wolves for Russian **tsars** and nobles.

Why the long face?

Thick fur on neck

Long and lanky body

Loves to run

| | ORIGIN: Russia | INTELLIGENCE | 🐾 🐾 🐾 🐾 🐾 |
| --- | --- | --- | --- |
| | COAT: Medium-length, wavy, silky | ENERGY LEVEL | 🐾 🐾 🐾 🐾 🐾 |
| LARGE | PERSONALITY: Calm and graceful | TRAINABILITY | 🐾 🐾 🐾 🐾 🐾 |

# Dachshund

Affectionately known as "sausage dogs", dachshunds are famous for their long bodies and little legs. They are a much-loved breed with a big personality. They are alert and loud, and make good little watchdogs.

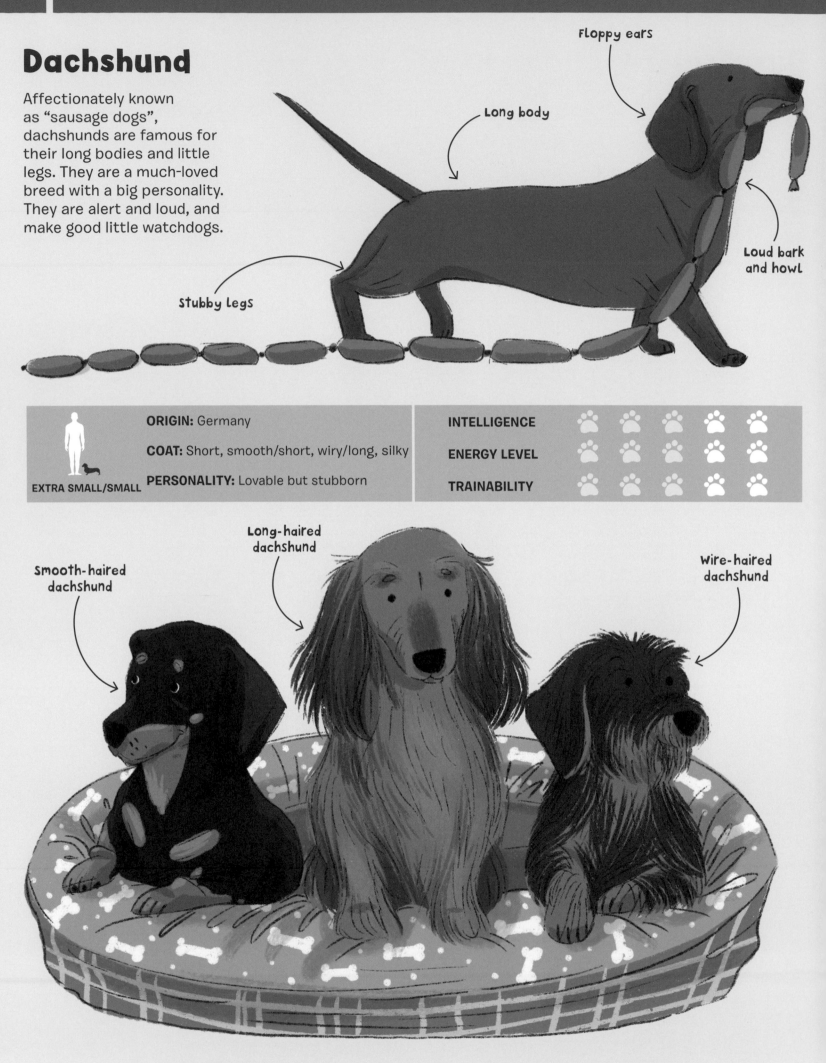

Long body

Floppy ears

Loud bark and howl

Stubby legs

**EXTRA SMALL/SMALL**

**ORIGIN:** Germany

**COAT:** Short, smooth/short, wiry/long, silky

**PERSONALITY:** Lovable but stubborn

| INTELLIGENCE | 🐾 🐾 🐾 🐾 🐾 |
| ENERGY LEVEL | 🐾 🐾 🐾 🐾 🐾 |
| TRAINABILITY | 🐾 🐾 🐾 🐾 🐾 |

Smooth-haired dachshund

Long-haired dachshund

Wire-haired dachshund

# Dandie Dinmont Terrier

These funny-looking little dogs have one of the lowest tums around! They were bred to fit down badger burrows, which helps to explain their long-and-low shape!

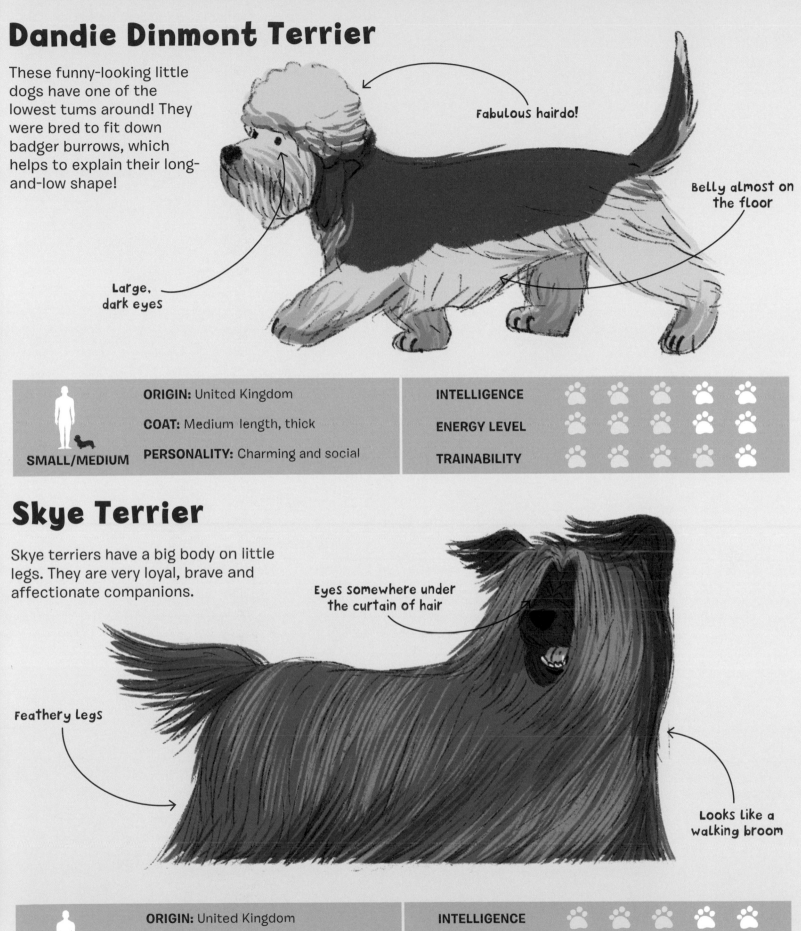

Fabulous hairdo!

Belly almost on the floor

Large, dark eyes

| | | INTELLIGENCE | 🐾 🐾 🐾 🐾 🐾 |
|---|---|---|---|
| **ORIGIN:** United Kingdom | | ENERGY LEVEL | 🐾 🐾 🐾 🐾 🐾 |
| **COAT:** Medium length, thick | | TRAINABILITY | 🐾 🐾 🐾 🐾 🐾 |
| **PERSONALITY:** Charming and social | | | |

SMALL/MEDIUM

# Skye Terrier

Skye terriers have a big body on little legs. They are very loyal, brave and affectionate companions.

Eyes somewhere under the curtain of hair

Feathery legs

Looks like a walking broom

| | | INTELLIGENCE | 🐾 🐾 🐾 🐾 🐾 |
|---|---|---|---|
| **ORIGIN:** United Kingdom | | ENERGY LEVEL | 🐾 🐾 🐾 🐾 🐾 |
| **COAT:** Long, silky | | TRAINABILITY | 🐾 🐾 🐾 🐾 🐾 |
| **PERSONALITY:** Loving and confident | | | |

MEDIUM

# Bichon Frisé

These fluffy little dogs have a personality as cuddly as their looks. They require a lot of grooming to get them looking their best, puffiest self.

often given a round haircut

Thick, white, curly coat

Black nose

| | | INTELLIGENCE | | | | | |
|---|---|---|---|---|---|---|---|
| **SMALL** | **ORIGIN:** The Canary Islands (Spain) | | | | | | |
| | **COAT:** Medium-length, curly | ENERGY LEVEL | | | | | |
| | **PERSONALITY:** Confident and affectionate | TRAINABILITY | | | | | |

# Keeshond

These gorgeous fluffy dogs were first used as watch-dogs on barge boats along the canals of the Netherlands. They are smart and easy to train.

Bushy tail

Thick, puffy mane

Black, grey and cream markings

| | | INTELLIGENCE | | | | | |
|---|---|---|---|---|---|---|---|
| **MEDIUM** | **ORIGIN:** The Netherlands | | | | | | |
| | **COAT:** Long, very thick | ENERGY LEVEL | | | | | |
| | **PERSONALITY:** Friendly and inquisitive | TRAINABILITY | | | | | |

# Pekingese

The Pekingese started off as a royal lapdog in China. It was only allowed to be owned by members of the Imperial Palace. They can be snooty with strangers but are loving towards their owners.

Flat face

Fuzzy everywhere!

Probably has legs somewhere under all that fur

|  EXTRA SMALL | ORIGIN: China | INTELLIGENCE | 🐾 🐾 🐾 🐾 🐾 |
|---|---|---|---|
| | COAT: Long, very thick | ENERGY LEVEL | 🐾 🐾 🐾 🐾 🐾 |
| | PERSONALITY: Charming and relaxed | TRAINABILITY | 🐾 🐾 🐾 🐾 🐾 |

# Chow Chow

Despite their fluffy appearance, chow chows aren't known for being the friendliest dogs. Though they can form close bonds with their owners, they aren't big cuddlers. They are usually quiet and suspicious of strangers.

A lion in disguise?

Scowling face

Thick, fleecy coat

| LARGE | ORIGIN: China | INTELLIGENCE | 🐾 🐾 🐾 🐾 🐾 |
|---|---|---|---|
| | COAT: Medium-length, very thick | ENERGY LEVEL | 🐾 🐾 🐾 🐾 🐾 |
| | PERSONALITY: Calm and independent | TRAINABILITY | 🐾 🐾 🐾 🐾 🐾 |

# Afghan Hound

This glamorous, ancient sighthound has an extra-long, silky coat, which would have originally protected them from extreme weather conditions in the mountains of Afghanistan.

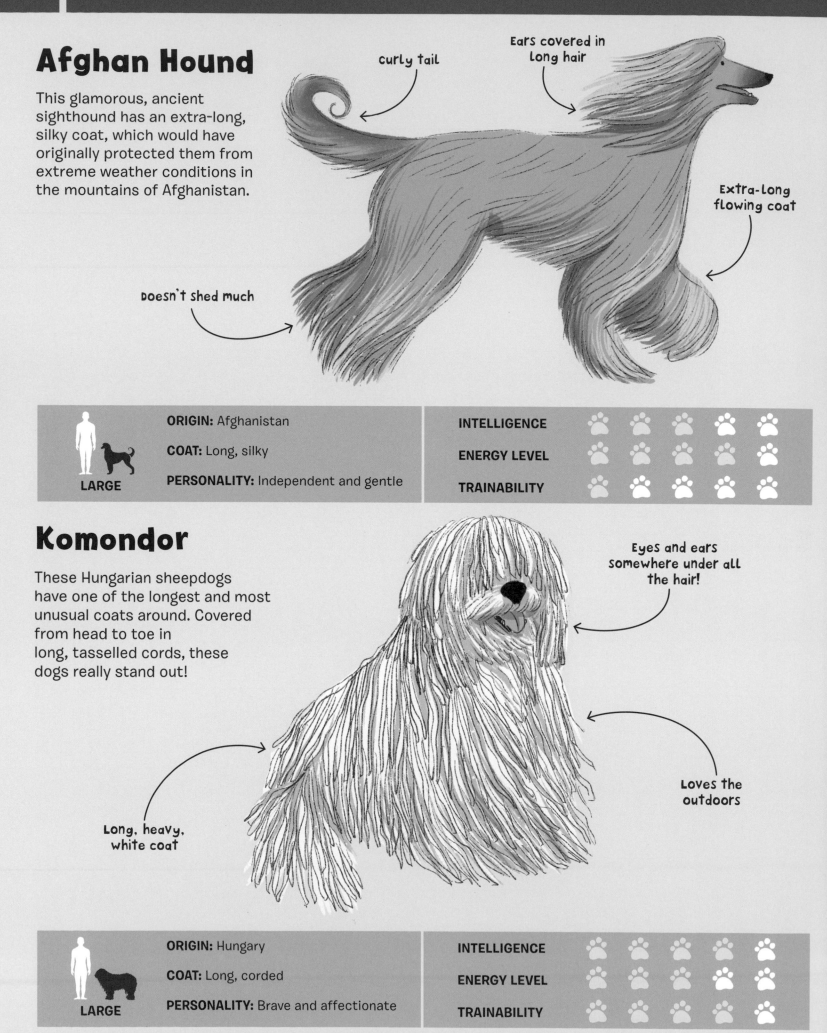

curly tail

Ears covered in Long hair

Extra-Long flowing coat

Doesn't shed much

| | | |
|---|---|---|
| **LARGE** | **ORIGIN:** Afghanistan | |
| | **COAT:** Long, silky | |
| | **PERSONALITY:** Independent and gentle | |

| | |
|---|---|
| INTELLIGENCE | 🐾🐾🐾🐾🐾 |
| ENERGY LEVEL | 🐾🐾🐾🐾🐾 |
| TRAINABILITY | 🐾🐾🐾🐾🐾 |

# Komondor

These Hungarian sheepdogs have one of the longest and most unusual coats around. Covered from head to toe in long, tasselled cords, these dogs really stand out!

Eyes and ears somewhere under all the hair!

Loves the outdoors

Long, heavy, white coat

| | | |
|---|---|---|
| **LARGE** | **ORIGIN:** Hungary | |
| | **COAT:** Long, corded | |
| | **PERSONALITY:** Brave and affectionate | |

| | |
|---|---|
| INTELLIGENCE | 🐾🐾🐾🐾🐾 |
| ENERGY LEVEL | 🐾🐾🐾🐾🐾 |
| TRAINABILITY | 🐾🐾🐾🐾🐾 |

# Yorkshire Terrier

You wouldn't think it from their beauty-pageant looks, but these little dogs were originally bred to catch rats in the mills and mines of Northern England. They are elegant but scrappy little dogs, with big personalities.

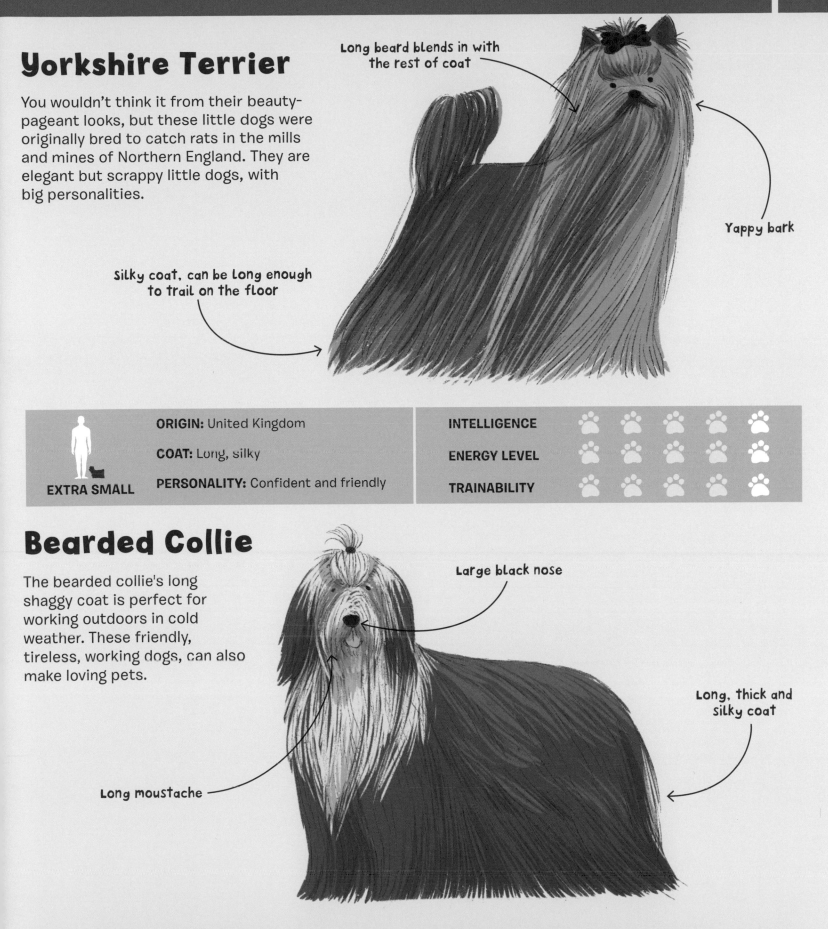

Long beard blends in with the rest of coat

Yappy bark

Silky coat, can be long enough to trail on the floor

| | |
|---|---|
| **ORIGIN:** United Kingdom | **INTELLIGENCE** 🐾🐾🐾🐾🐾 |
| **COAT:** Long, silky | **ENERGY LEVEL** 🐾🐾🐾🐾🐾 |
| EXTRA SMALL    **PERSONALITY:** Confident and friendly | **TRAINABILITY** 🐾🐾🐾🐾🐾 |

# Bearded Collie

The bearded collie's long shaggy coat is perfect for working outdoors in cold weather. These friendly, tireless, working dogs, can also make loving pets.

Large black nose

Long, thick and silky coat

Long moustache

| | |
|---|---|
| **ORIGIN:** United Kingdom | **INTELLIGENCE** 🐾🐾🐾🐾🐾 |
| **COAT:** Long, silky, thick | **ENERGY LEVEL** 🐾🐾🐾🐾🐾 |
| MEDIUM/LARGE    **PERSONALITY:** Playful and affectionate | **TRAINABILITY** 🐾🐾🐾🐾🐾 |

# Bedlington Terrier

These fluffy terriers look like little lambs. Their traditional **"show clip"** gives them an unusual, curved head shape. They are speedy, athletic and caring dogs, with a big bark.

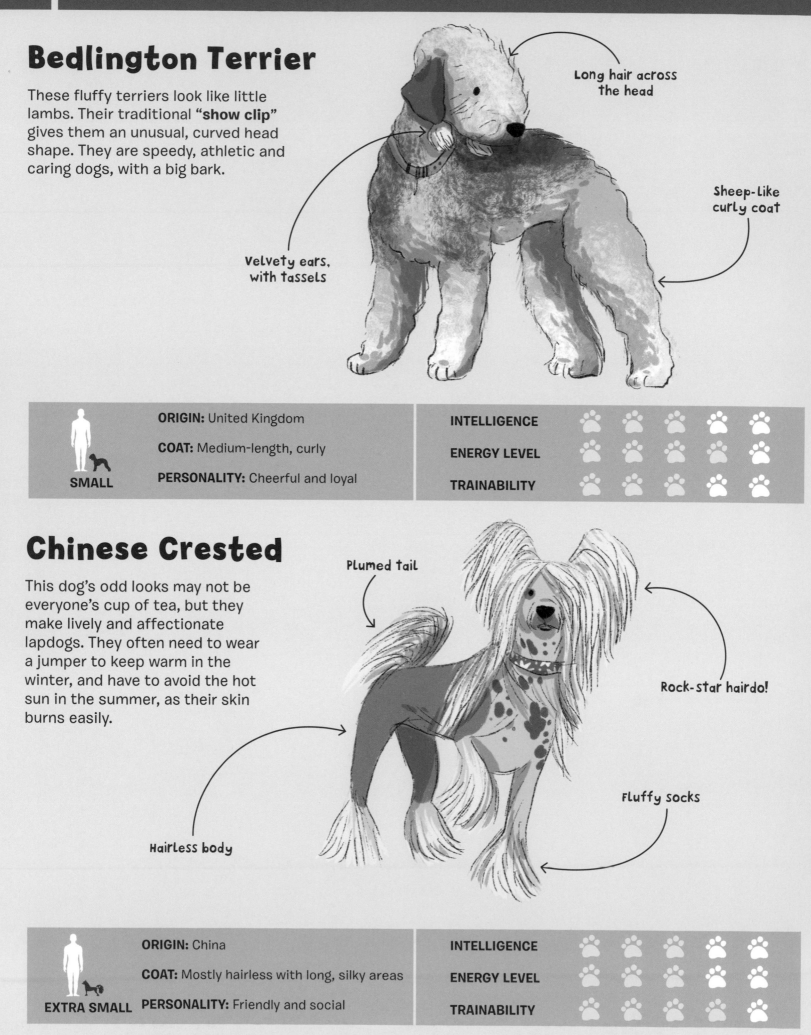

Long hair across the head

Sheep-like curly coat

Velvety ears, with tassels

**ORIGIN:** United Kingdom

**COAT:** Medium-length, curly

**PERSONALITY:** Cheerful and loyal

**SMALL**

INTELLIGENCE

ENERGY LEVEL

TRAINABILITY

# Chinese Crested

This dog's odd looks may not be everyone's cup of tea, but they make lively and affectionate lapdogs. They often need to wear a jumper to keep warm in the winter, and have to avoid the hot sun in the summer, as their skin burns easily.

Plumed tail

Rock-star hairdo!

Fluffy socks

Hairless body

**ORIGIN:** China

**COAT:** Mostly hairless with long, silky areas

**EXTRA SMALL** **PERSONALITY:** Friendly and social

INTELLIGENCE

ENERGY LEVEL

TRAINABILITY

# Poodle

The dog best known for its fancy haircuts has to be the poodle! Many owners like to clip and groom their pet's fur into all kinds of different shapes. However, there is much more to poodles than their looks! They are one of the most intelligent dog breeds.

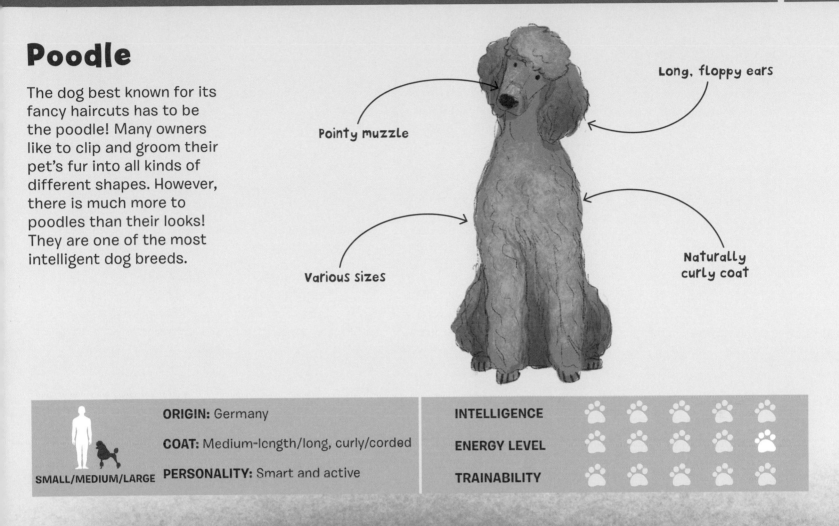

Pointy muzzle

Long, floppy ears

Various sizes

Naturally curly coat

**ORIGIN:** Germany

**COAT:** Medium-length/long, curly/corded

**PERSONALITY:** Smart and active

SMALL/MEDIUM/LARGE

INTELLIGENCE

ENERGY LEVEL

TRAINABILITY

## Poodle Haircuts

continental clip

corded poodle

Puppy clip

# Dalmatian

This dog is hard to miss, thanks to its iconic spotty coat. Each Dalmatian's coat is unique, with a different pattern and number of spots. Puppies are born completely white, with their spots starting to show after a few weeks.

Dalmatians have a history of working as "coach dogs", they would trot alongside carriages to protect the people inside and their horses from robbers. Today, they make loyal family pets.

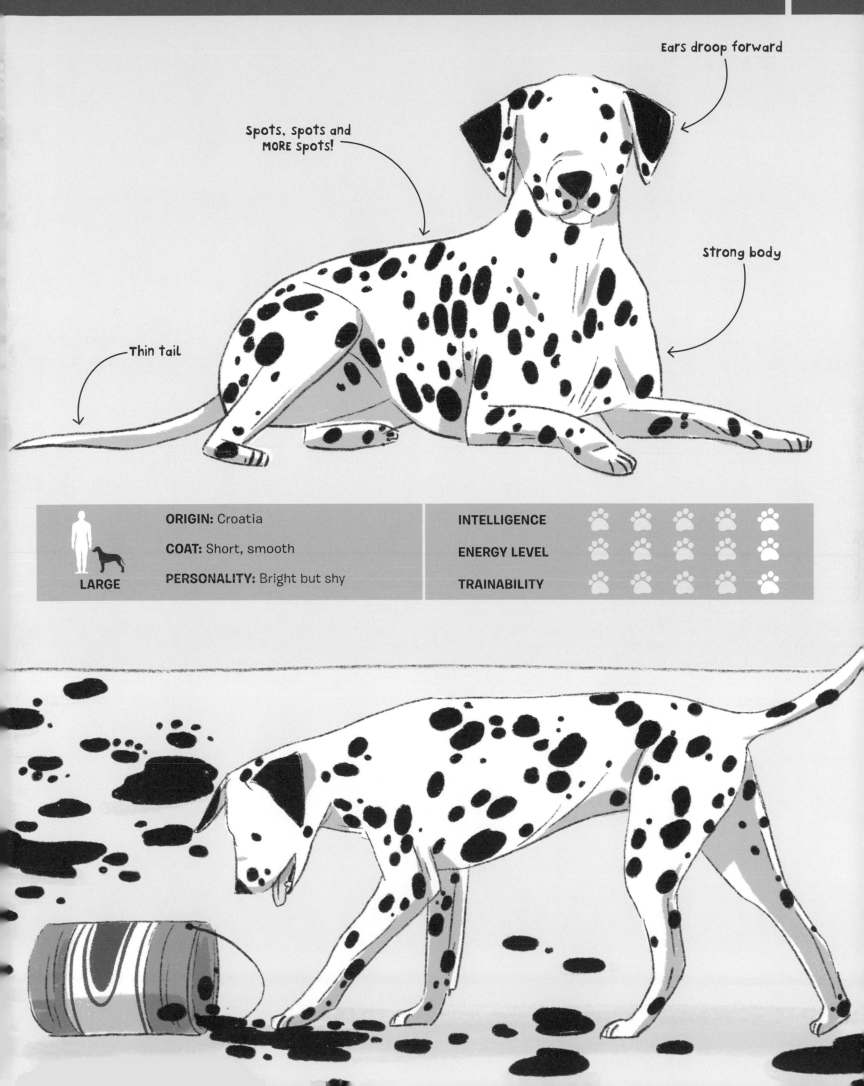

Ears droop forward

Spots, spots and MORE spots!

strong body

Thin tail

**ORIGIN:** Croatia

**COAT:** Short, smooth

**PERSONALITY:** Bright but shy

**LARGE**

INTELLIGENCE

ENERGY LEVEL

TRAINABILITY

# Pharaoh Hound

The Pharaoh Hound is actually a fairly modern breed, but it bears a very strong resemblance to dogs shown in artwork from ancient Egypt. They are elegant, graceful dogs that can make playful and loving pets.

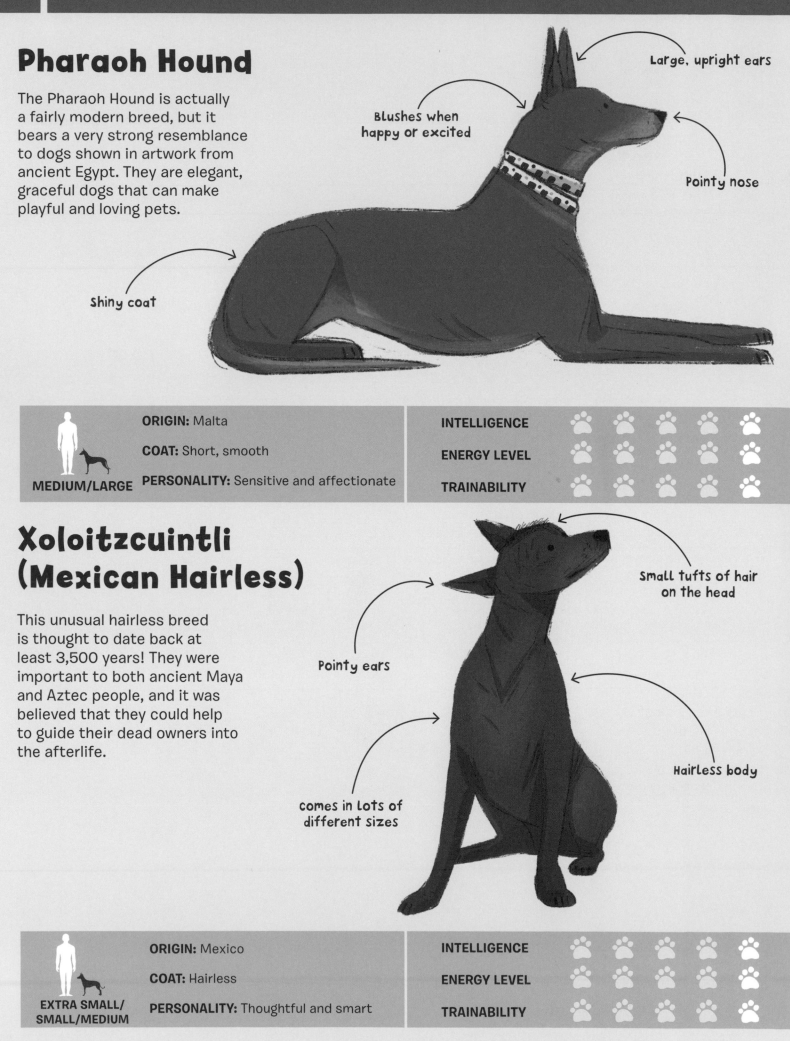

Large, upright ears

Blushes when happy or excited

Pointy nose

Shiny coat

**ORIGIN:** Malta

**COAT:** Short, smooth

**PERSONALITY:** Sensitive and affectionate

**MEDIUM/LARGE**

INTELLIGENCE

ENERGY LEVEL

TRAINABILITY

# Xoloitzcuintli (Mexican Hairless)

This unusual hairless breed is thought to date back at least 3,500 years! They were important to both ancient Maya and Aztec people, and it was believed that they could help to guide their dead owners into the afterlife.

Small tufts of hair on the head

Pointy ears

comes in Lots of different sizes

Hairless body

**ORIGIN:** Mexico

**COAT:** Hairless

**PERSONALITY:** Thoughtful and smart

**EXTRA SMALL/ SMALL/MEDIUM**

INTELLIGENCE

ENERGY LEVEL

TRAINABILITY

# New Guinea Singing Dog

This ancient breed is closely related to the Australian dingo. As their name suggests, they have a special talent for "singing". They have tuneful, yodel-like howls, and sometimes "sing" together, in a chorus. They mostly live semi-wild, so don't make easy pets.

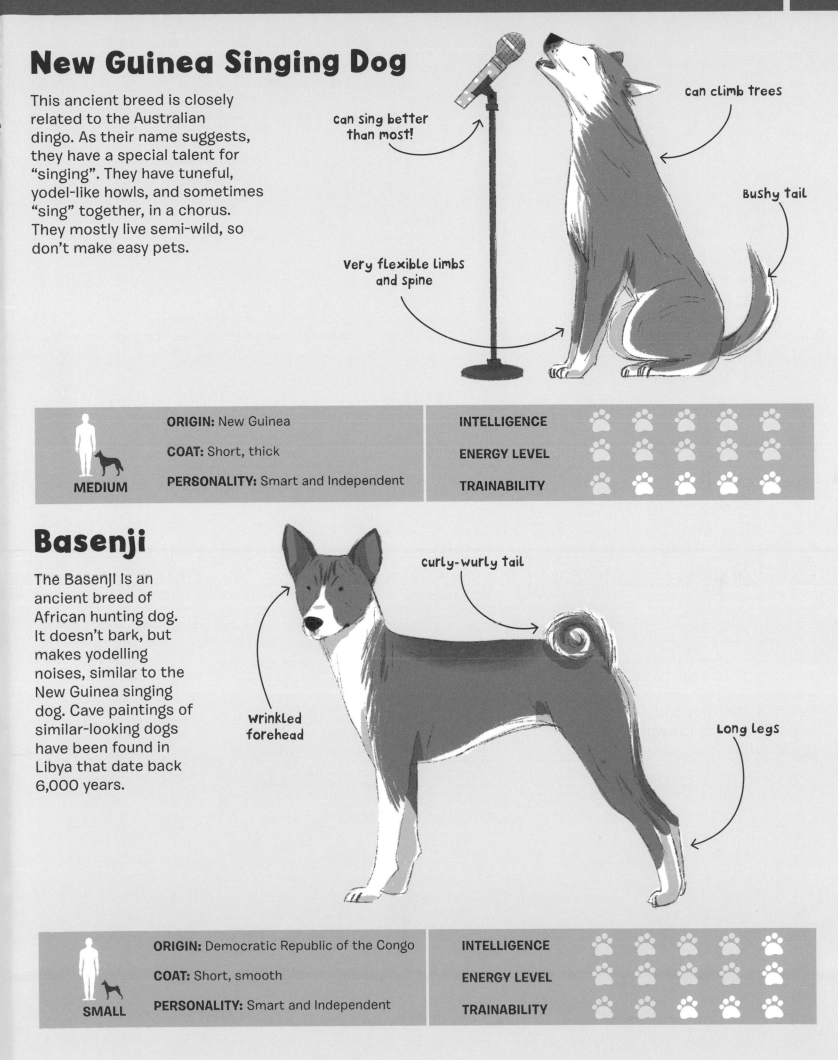

can sing better than most!

can climb trees

Bushy tail

Very flexible limbs and spine

**MEDIUM**

**ORIGIN:** New Guinea

**COAT:** Short, thick

**PERSONALITY:** Smart and Independent

INTELLIGENCE

ENERGY LEVEL

TRAINABILITY

# Basenji

The Basenji is an ancient breed of African hunting dog. It doesn't bark, but makes yodelling noises, similar to the New Guinea singing dog. Cave paintings of similar-looking dogs have been found in Libya that date back 6,000 years.

curly-wurly tail

wrinkled forehead

Long legs

**SMALL**

**ORIGIN:** Democratic Republic of the Congo

**COAT:** Short, smooth

**PERSONALITY:** Smart and Independent

INTELLIGENCE

ENERGY LEVEL

TRAINABILITY

# GLOSSARY

**Agility (dog sport)** – a sport where dogs complete complicated obstacle courses, including objects that they have run through, around, under, or jump over.

**Burrows** – holes or tunnels dug by animals.

**Corded** – a type of dog coat that forms into long rope-like strands, similar to dreadlocks.

**Crossbreeding** – when two dogs of different breeds have puppies.

**Descendants** – people or animals that are related to an individual or group who lived in the past. For example, you are a descendant of your parents and grandparents.

**Detection dogs** – dogs that are trained to use their senses (usually smell) to detect items, such as explosives and illegal drugs. They are also known as sniffer dogs.

**Domesticate** – to be tamed or trained to live or work with humans.

**Endurance** – the ability or strength to continue doing something for a long time.

**Genetically** – genetics shows how our genes carry information from parents to children

**Lapdogs** – dogs that are small enough to sit on someone's lap and make friendly companions.

**Nomadic** – nomadic people move around from place to place, with no fixed home.

**Puffins** – black and white seabirds that nest in holes and caves along coastal cliffs.

**Purebreds** – dogs belonging to a specific breed, not a crossbreed or mongrel.

**Ranches** – large farms for raising horses, cattle or sheep (usually in Mexico, Western United States or Western Canada).

**Rehoming shelter** – a place where dogs (or other animals) who were lost, stray, or given up by their owners, are looked after until they can be adopted into a new home.

**Service dog (or assistance dog)** – a dog that has been trained to assist a person with a disability. Examples of service dogs include guide dogs, hearing dogs, medical response dogs and autism service dogs.

**Show clip** – a haircut or style used on dogs that compete in dog shows.

**Therapy dog** – dogs that are trained to provide comfort and support to people. Unlike service dogs (see above) who only assist one person, therapy dogs help multiple individuals, or groups of people. They often work in hospitals, schools, or nursing and retirement homes.

**Truffle** – a strong-smelling edible fungus that grows underground. They are expensive because they are very rare.

**Tsar** – a Russian emperor, before 1917.

**Underbite (or undershot)** – when the lower jaw or teeth stick out in front of the upper jaw or teeth, when the mouth is closed.

**Wiry** – a type of dog coat that is rough, thick and bristly.

# INDEX

## ABOUT THE AUTHOR

Annabel is a writer and artist based in Cornwall, UK. Having worked as a bookseller for many years, she now writes children's books focusing on animals and the natural world. Her recent titles include *What Can I See in the Wild?*, *Seasons* and *The Spectacular Lives of Sharks*.

## ABOUT THE ILLUSTRATOR

Marina is a talented illustrator of children's books from Ukraine. Her stunning illustrations are inspired by her own childhood, children, nature, magical moments and fairytales.

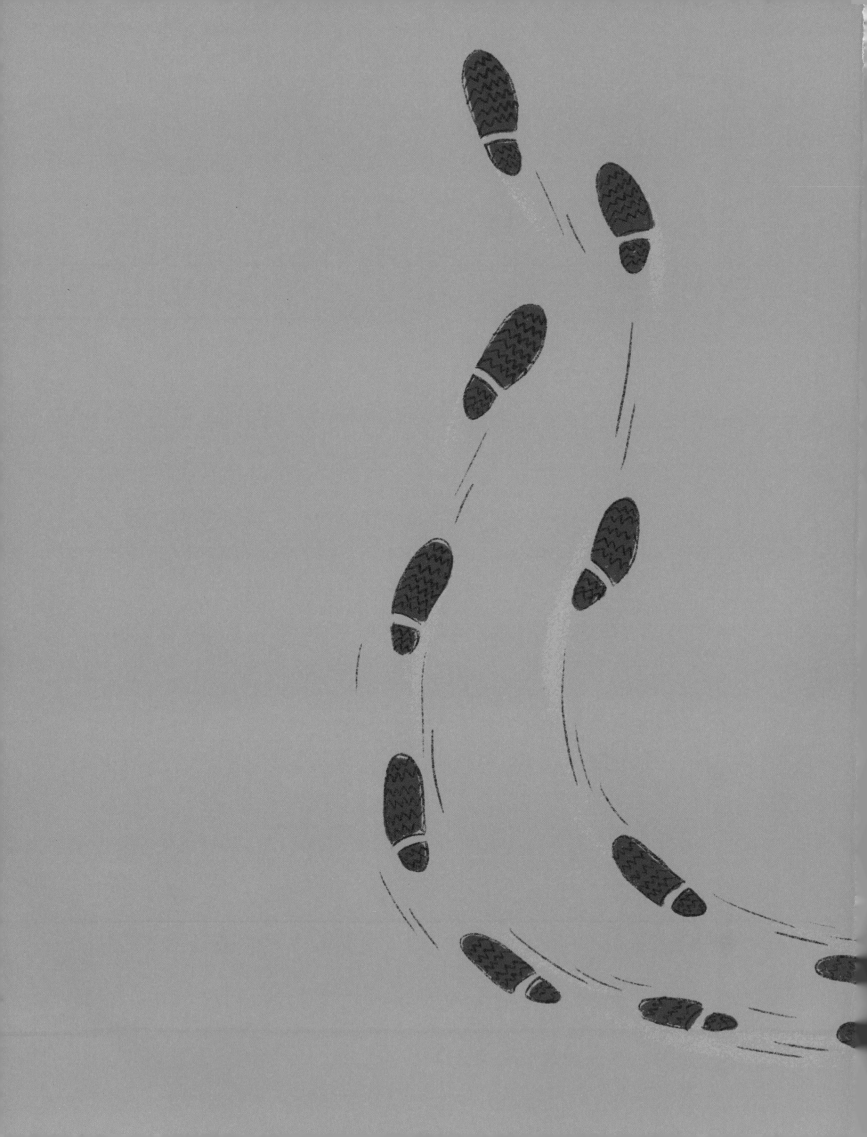